STEVEN: A RUNNER'S LIFE

AN ULTRARUNNER'S JOURNEY

JENNIE McNEAL

BALBOA.PRESS
A DIVISION OF HAY HOUSE

Balboa Press books may be ordered through booksellers or by contacting:

Balboa Press
A Division of Hay House
1663 Liberty Drive
Bloomington, IN 47403
www.balboapress.com
1 (877) 407-4847

Because of the dynamic nature of the Internet, any web addresses or
links contained in this book may have changed since publication and
may no longer be valid. The views expressed in this work are solely those
of the author and do not necessarily reflect the views of the publisher,
and the publisher hereby disclaims any responsibility for them.

The author of this book does not dispense medical advice or prescribe the use
of any technique as a form of treatment for physical, emotional, or medical
problems without the advice of a physician, either directly or indirectly. The
intent of the author is only to offer information of a general nature to help
you in your quest for emotional and spiritual well-being. In the event you use
any of the information in this book for yourself, which is your constitutional
right, the author and the publisher assume no responsibility for your actions.

Any people depicted in stock imagery provided by Getty Images are
models, and such images are being used for illustrative purposes only.
Certain stock imagery © Getty Images.

Print information available on the last page.

ISBN: 978-1-9822-4003-5 (sc)
ISBN: 978-1-9822-4004-2 (e)

Library of Congress Control Number: 2019920684

Balboa Press rev. date: 12/12/2019

To all those who have a dream and
pursue it with all their heart.

I can do all things through Christ who strengthens me.

—Philippians 4:13 (NKJV)

Steven's life verse

ACKNOWLEDGMENTS

I want to thank all of the friends of Steven in his running groups over the years—especially the NRC RunWILD in Nashville who felt like family to him. Also, I am grateful to the 12th South running group and to Joanna, who kept the group together after Steven left Nashville to pursue his running dream. To those members of the East Nasty running group who always come through for each other and make him feel welcome every time he's with them, thank you.

Thanks to the NRC-Nashville Running Company crew—especially to Lee Wilson, who allowed Steven to dream big and inspired him to go to Oregon, his home state.

And gratitude to all of the people who have been a member of his support team or crew over the years—Daniel, Jeff, Beth, and Jonathan for the help at the Bear 100 mile and Shannon and Erik for hosting them at the Bear. Special thanks to his bud, Mayne, who met him out west for hikes and still hosts him in Nashville whenever he is there. Thank you to Daniel and Casey for pacing and helping at the Bryce Canyon 100 mile. And thank you to Melissa, Emma and Joanna for coming to France and being with him as support at the Ultra-Trail du Mont-Blanc.

Special thanks to our daughter and son-in-law, Amy and Dillon, who went above and beyond in prayers and help with communication to us about the races. I love you both. And thank you to Dillon for going to Steven's first 100-mile race, the Bear 100 in Idaho, where there was an epic storm that knocked out GPS communication. But with God's help and word of mouth of other runners on the trail, Dillon still found Steven at a remote lodge at mile 75.

And forever gratitude to my husband, Jay, who drove us to all of Steven's races we could possibly attend and sailed with me to England and rode multiple trains to Chamonix, France. He sat outside with me in freezing weather while waiting for Steven at aid stations at many races, especially Wisconsin and Utah and Oregon. Thank you for driving extra times so I could write in my journals. I love you.

And to Steven, this thanks is for you. You have inspired me and so many others with your unfailing pursuit of your dreams. May God richly bless you for your whole life with love and happiness. I love you.

And to our Lord Jesus Christ, who knew us before we were even formed and is the whole reason this was possible, thank you.

And to all those who read this book, prayers and blessings to all of you.

STEVEN'S PREFACE

"Do you sleep?" This is a question I often get from inquisitive, wide-eyed new acquaintances if they learn that I run in 100-mile trail-running events. "What do you eat? "What are your paces like for that distance?" All fair and good questions, but it's impossible to get to the heart of these type of events just by prying in with a few surface inquiries about extraneous details.

Just like anything in life that you become passionate about, trail running for me became more than just an activity, an exercise, and a segment of my day. It became an almost all-encompassing lifestyle. What started as barely running a mile and working up to my first 5k race, eventually became weekend excursions with friends in the mountains training for hours and days on end to prepare for multi-day events in extreme conditions.

I remember training for my first 100 miler, a total unknown beast of an event for which I had no idea what I needed to be prepared. Leaving a burrito dinner with friends on a Saturday evening, I geared up and went for a training run at a local hilly park, headlamp in hand. My goal was to run through the night until sun-up, as I knew my 100-mile event would require me to run through an entire night. My stomach rebelled on the first 11-mile loop of this training session (thanks burritos). It was July in Tennessee, so I had hopes that I would avoid the heat since it was a night run, but it was very humid and warm. My close training buddy Daniel joined me in the middle of the night (with coffee!) for loop two, which helped ease me through miles 11-22. Loop three was rough, as I was alone again and quite tired. But I kept moving forward, slowly, and eventually the sun came up as I was finishing my 33-mile night run. "Embrace the crazy", I told myself. That was one of my mantras during training. I had a doctor friend who advised me against such a night run, because the body needs sleep. What he didn't understand is that I also needed the mental training.

So much of what we do in life we confine to parameters that aren't broad enough. Just as a person doesn't get chosen for a job based solely on test scores or their resume, a person doesn't complete or do well in a running event merely because they are trained well physically. There are mental, emotional and even spiritual factors at work there also. At almost any ultramarathon event, you are virtually guaranteed to have a low point physically. How you handle the crisis can often determine the ultimate outcome.

The parallels between ultrarunning and life have taught me so much, and for that I am thankful. One of those parallels is that we all need other people in our lives sometimes to help us along our journey. I've had some great crew members to support me at a lot of my races, including my wonderful, up-for-almost-anything parents. They've braved the cold and wind often standing at aid stations for hours waiting to see me for a few brief moments. And to have a Mom who put together a book about my crazy trail and life antics, I really am truly blessed.

I hope that for anyone reading this book, the stories told here will remind you of similar good times that were hard earned but yielded dividends, and that it will encourage or inspire you to reach further within yourself than you think is possible. I promise you it won't be easy. But it will be worth it.

CHAPTER 1

A Rough Beginning

When was the last time you had a conversation that changed your life?

Possibly when you had an interview with a college admissions counselor and decided your major? Perhaps when you decided on the path your life would take for the next twenty or thirty years? Or when your best friend asked you to get married?

One of mine was when I was nearly sixty years old and our son said, "I'm going to run in a 50-mile race." This was said about a year and a half after he ran his first marathon (26.2 miles)—the St. Jude Country Music Marathon—in eighty-degree heat and collapsed at mile 21. Unbeknownst to us, he had to be taken by ambulance to one of the local hospitals, where he was rehydrated by IV in the ER.

To make things even worse, Steven didn't have his cell phone with him and couldn't remember my cell phone number because his contacts are listed by name. When he got to the ER, he did remember my work number at the hospital laboratory in Rome, Georgia. So the Nashville hospital nurse called my work number. A really kind nurse friend of mine stayed on the phone line with him for twenty to thirty minutes while a lab friend found my cell phone number in her address book.

Finally he was able to contact me through my phone while I was standing on a bridge between the Tennessee Titans stadium and the Schermerhorn Symphony Center (where Steven worked the first nine years he lived in Nashville). Jay, my husband, and I had walked around the entire stadium twice in hopes of finding Steven. When I got his call, even though he was in the ER, it was wonderful to hear his voice and know where he was and that he was being taken care of. His girlfriend at the time was a nurse and was with him.

When Jay and I located the ER, we went inside and waited until the staff had given Steven enough fluids to rehydrate him. The doctor checked him and said he could be released to go home. We followed Steven and his girlfriend back to his condo. Then we went to Quizno's to get sandwiches for them to eat and brought them back to the condo. After everyone had gotten some food, his girlfriend said she would stay and watch over Steven so that we could drive back home to Georgia. It was a real comfort to know she would be there with him.

All this information about his first attempt at a regular 26.2-mile marathon is to say that, when he said, "I'm going to run in a 50-mile race," my mind was going over and over all the details of what had happened then. And what could he possibly be thinking about running almost twice as far?

Little did I know that this was just the beginning of several years on a journey to see him in races in different states and, eventually, to different countries. Jeremiah 29:11 says, "I know the plans I have for you, says the Lord, plans to prosper you and not to harm you; plans to give you hope and a future" (NIV). God wants us to trust Him. He didn't say it would be easy.

CHAPTER 2

Why He Runs

Reasons by Steven McNeal
September 2015

I sometimes wonder, *Why do I run?* Only sometimes, but I do wonder occasionally. Can I answer why in a blog post? Maybe on some level, but no explanation I could put into words alone would do complete justice to all my reasons. Can words explain the feeling I get when I succeed in reaching my goals at a race I've worked toward for months? Or feelings I get when I fail? Can words appropriately describe the ins and outs of the countless relationships that have developed for me through running groups or capture the meaning of the seemingly mundane sensations on runs, such as seeing yet another deer in the woods or looking up at the stars in the predawn hours? What about the building anticipation and intensified sense of life I experience when approaching a race or weekend running excursion with friends? Nah, words can't really capture any of those things with the apropos spirit.

Before I ran ultras, I used to play music. For me music was similar to running. Playing connected me with a larger community, working toward common goals together. And on an individual level, you could pour yourself out into the pursuit of musical skill and approaching the perfection of honing your craft, just as you can in running. And always, as I was involved in the music realm, I had a deep yearning to express myself in ways I couldn't with mere words. Sometimes I wanted to shout through my instrument to express the intensity of my heart, and sometimes I wanted to play a cathartic whisper.

When people hear that I run ultras or especially that I have run 100-mile races, they often ask, "Why?" I have, for years, wanted to create a video in a feeble attempt to have a legitimate response to people when they ask that question. I've contemplated the music I would use, the cinematography to capture the essence, and the dialogue to accompany and complete the production. This idea pushed me to buy a GoPro camera, and, since that purchase, I've made almost twenty videos but not the one titled, "Why I Run."

Why haven't I followed through on the whole reason I started making running videos? Why would I prioritize other projects over the one that initially led to inspiration? I think, it's because the reasons I run are so deep, so sacred to me, that I can't create something that doesn't do those reasons the best justice that I can possibly do. I have an insatiable desire to create. To communicate those deep thoughts and feelings that can't be expressed with statements. So, one of these days, I will make that video. One of these days I'll be able to *show* people why I run.

In the meantime, I'm going to run. And I'm going to make other running videos of different trails and groups that are such a huge part of the reason why I run. *And* I'm going to start working on a huge video project that I'm *really* excited about—a documentary that really resonates with me and why I run. More details to come on that! My reasons for all of this, are simply this: I have an irresistible urge, an insatiable compulsion to create. To express. To experience this running lifestyle and share it with others in a way that helps, at least on some level, to reconcile the insane miles and routines of our running culture to fulfilling experiences. And some day, maybe I can show you. And you will see and truly hear why I run.

***

Mom's *note: Steven did make a video of his first 100-mile race, the Bear 100, and it remains my favorite. In order to view it go to YouTube and select "2014 Bear 100-Epic weather" by Steven McNeal. It lasts 10:42 minutes and explains much of what happened there.)*

CHAPTER 3

The Bear 100

In June 2014, Steven and his friends Daniel, Beth, and Lee were running in a three-day race called the Chattanooga Stage Race. On day 1, the runners run 22 miles on Lookout Mountain. On day 2, they run 18 miles on Raccoon Mountain. And on day 3, they run 20 miles on Signal Mountain. The winner is determined from combining the best times from all three runs.

Jay and I went to the Lookout Mountain race on day 1. When Steven finished that day, he told us he was considering entering his first hundred-mile race, the Bear 100 around Bear Lake in Utah and ending in Idaho on September 26 to 27. I just stood there, mostly in shock, among people running through the finish line at the stage race, no longer really seeing or hearing what was going.

Beth and Daniel had finished and came over to say hello to us. Beth said, "What do you think about Steven running in the Bear 100?"

All I could think of to say was, "He's an adult and can make his own decisions." But I felt totally unprepared to respond. It would take a lot of hours in prayer before I could accept it.

It turned out that Beth was on Steven's crew for the Bear, and Daniel was his pace runner.

God bless them both! They're wonderful! I don't believe he would have been able to complete that race without them.

Steven wrote a partial blog of his experiences during the "Bear" and titled it "100 Miles of Fun [kind of]:

> "I never want to do a 100." I vividly remember these words exiting my mouth immediately following a cold, rainy, muddy day spent

running the Lookout Mountain 50-mile trail run in Chattanooga, Tennessee, in December 2013. I had prepared rigorously for that race, and the elements, combined with some poor nutrition choices, left me struggling to finish, and at a much slower pace than I had hoped for. Flash forward to September 26, 2014, and I somehow find myself at the start line of the Bear 100 in Logan, Utah.

It had been a grueling, strength-sapping summer of training. I had a solid base and quickly hit 70-plus-mile weeks in June and July, finally peaking in one of the hottest Augusts on record with 80-mile weeks. Training, in the 100-miler training sense, is basically keeping your body on the verge of utter exhaustion at all times. You're trying to wrap your head around how one can possibly cover 100 miles through the mountains on foot at one go, especially you. So you string together a series of training runs and weeks that seem borderline insane and supplement with as much eating and sleeping as possible. Much of the time, I trained with my friend Jeff Davis, who talked me into this seemingly reckless but oddly enticing undertaking. One weekend, Jeff and I met up in the Smoky Mountains for a 35-mile training jaunt on the AT, which culminated with me barely being able to hike the last 8 miles, as I kept having to toss back up any water or food that just wouldn't stay down. A few weeks later, I bonked again after doing several doubles (two-a-day runs) and joined Jeff for a 10-mile run on one of the most humid mornings. I felt miserable, but this time I at least made it home before getting sick. Long story short ... I was ready.

Average high temperatures for the Bear 100 course in late September are low seventies. In 2013, it was snowy and icy. When Jeff and I lined up for the race, it was muggy and sixty-four degrees, with temperatures quickly on the rise. Race start at 6:00 a.m. came and went, and we were off and running in the predawn dark. The first mile or so was fairly flat, with gentle inclines through neighborhoods on the roads. Before we knew it, we were on a steadily rising trail up the first 5-mile climb, in a conga line of 340 other runners turned hikers. Most of the people around me were silent, focusing on our slow but steady rhythm up the mountain and soaking in the first of two sunrises for most of this event. After leveling off a few times, climbing some more, going through bright yellow aspen forests and sparse rocky mountain-side trails, I arrived at the first aid station at mile 10.4.

Arriving at aid stations in a race of this length is akin to finishing a school year as a kid. You know there is an end in sight and when it should theoretically arrive, but it often seems elusive and impossibly far away. When you finally reach one, the brief respite and relief at having actual proof of progress are blissful. I stopped for about five minutes at that first aid station, taking in some food and water and chatting briefly with a guy from Florida who was wearing a Lookout 50-miler shirt—the same race that I had done in Chattanooga.

Once I got moving, I settled in to a steady pace, a nice easy jog on flats and runnable downhills, and hiking a sustainable pace on any noticeable uphill climbs. The temperature was really starting to rise as time went on, and I passed the aid station at mile 19.6. About 30 miles out of the 100 were dirt and gravel roads, with much of those being between miles 20 to 40. Those miles happened to be in the heat of the day for me, and running on really exposed dirt roads under a punishing sun is not my idea of a good time. When I reached an aid station at mile 22.5, I happened to see that the temperature on my Garmin showed 90 degrees. I think it overestimates, but after the race, I saw that it had recorded a high temp of 100.4! Needless to say, I was starting to feel it.

Shortly after 2:00 p.m., I arrived at Cowley Canyon, an aid station at mile 30, where my awesome friends (aka crew), Daniel Hudgins, Beth Meadows, and Jonathan Minton, cheered me in. This was the first point of several where I knew I would see my crew, which gives a huge boost and allowed me to sit and just let them take care of me. Shortly, after wolfing down some watermelon, pretzels, and whatever else they brought to me in my lawn chair, I got moving again.

I was now in the heat of the day, and almost immediately after leaving that aid station, on more sun-soaking dirt roads, I noticed that I wasn't feeling well. My legs were getting a little tired, but more importantly, the effects of the heat were really getting to me. I felt unnecessarily sluggish and fatigued. I could tell I was starting to have a hard time digesting food as my body flushed blood to the surface, away from the stomach, in an attempt to avoid overheating. As a few miles passed and I knew I needed more fuel, I tried forcing a bite of a Honey Stinger waffle down but couldn't get it down. At some point in this time period, I had an interesting temporary distraction when I heard some wild sheep baaing *really* close by. What struck me was how loud their calls were. I rounded a bend and suddenly found myself face to face with a line of about five or more of them about to cross the trail directly in front of me! Both the sheep and I stopped in our tracks, staring at each other and waiting to see who moved first. I guess I won the stare down, as the lead sheep turned around, and they retreated back from where they had come from.

My level of discomfort continued to rise after the encounter with the sheep. I wasn't doing much running even on flat ground at this point, and my body even hurt while merely hiking. I remember my whole body aching painfully, so bad that I literally almost curled up in a ball on the side of the trail. I was probably around mile 34 at that point, and I was beginning to seriously doubt if I could finish.

Continuing in that level of pain would have been sheer torture. But what would all my friends who'd bought flights out there think? And all the people back home? How would I feel about myself if I dropped? I tried not to think about the potential repercussions too much. Suddenly and not entirely unexpectedly I got so sick that I lost everything I had taken in over the last few hours. I didn't know it at the time, but it was the beginning of a gradual turning point for the better.

Several people who passed when I was at those lower points stopped or slowed down to ask if I needed anything, which was awesome, One guy in particular saw me, and he really encouraged me by telling me that this was his tenth 100, and he had been through it all. He asked me if I remembered what the elevation profile of the course looked like (think really intense electrocardiogram), and he said the way I felt both physically and emotionally in the race would be like that. I would have high points and low points, but things wouldn't always stay low. He advised me to just get to the next aid station and take some time there to cool off and get some calories back in. It was very slow moving, but after what seemed like forever, I finally did reach that aid station at mile 36.9, where I sat for about ten or fifteen minutes and got down some chicken noodle soup. The next spot where I would see my crew was mile 45, so I knew I had to get there. So off I went, not knowing how my body was going to feel and respond over the next miles.

It was getting later in the afternoon, and while it was still hot, I could feel the beginnings of a break in the heat. There was a split in the trail at one point with no markings on which way to go, so I backtracked until I found the nearest runner, who happened to be a sixty-something year old man. It's amazing to see how hardy some people can be at an older age! We stuck together for maybe ten minutes or so until we saw course markings, letting us know we were on course, and I pulled back ahead. At one point, I was running alongside a healthy stream, and I stopped and soaked my head in the cool water. Shortly thereafter, I began to feel some strength returning (finally!). With a gradual downhill into the aid at 45, I was able to pick up speed and run steadily to the aid station.

My crew had expected me hours earlier at mile 45, so when I arrived, it took me a minute to find one of them. Daniel was still waiting at the tent and found me and immediately helped me start refueling with what eventually became my miracle nutrition strategy for the race—chicken noodle soup or broth and potato chips! I think that diet ended up being the perfect combination of carbs, sodium, hydration, and fats that my body needed for the long haul. Eventually, Beth and Jonathan made it over to the tent and checked in on me. This is when I found out that Jeff had also been struggling some and had gotten sick as well. After taking in as much as my stomach would allow, Jonathan walked me over to the trail to continue the journey in the dimming twilight.

Leaving there, I had to start with my headlamp on, for what would be many hours of running through the night, The first few hours of the night "run" was mostly hiking for miles up one of the longest climbs on the course, rising from around 5,000 feet of elevation to over 8,000 in four or five miles. I wasn't sure how my body was going to hold up, even though I had continued to feel better leaving that aid station at mile 45. Fortunately, the temps were now in the sixties or seventies, and I was feeling strong enough to maintain a steady long training run effort pace. Miles passed relatively uneventfully, and eventually I passed through the aid station at mile 51, stopping to sip some coveted but gross coffee (the only aid station I found coffee in the entire race) and down some lukewarm broth. At least the conversation with some of the volunteers was nice.

Next I had a long stretch to cover to get to the subsequent aid station at mile 61. This was probably the loneliest section for me, which was amplified by the dark and sparseness of other runners at this later point. Making new friends with other runners you encounter with headlamps at night hardly seems appropriate, but I did have a few brief interactions. I remember reaching a hefty stream with another runner at one point, and we had to wade through thigh-deep water for a few minutes trying to find where the trail continued. We figured it out and, eventually and after another few hours, I reached mile 61 and the next aid station.

Daniel was waiting for me in a group around a cozy campfire beside the aid tent at mile 61. He offered for me to sit by the fire while he grabbed food for me, but that wasn't appealing to me because I was still a little warm, with the humidity in the air from the approaching storm front. Jeff and I had gotten farther apart in the race at this point, so Beth and Jonathan were somewhere farther along on the course helping him out. Daniel was in his running gear ready to run with me from this point, which was part of our plan. Before we left the aid station, it started raining—hard. Those around the campfire moved to huddle underneath the station tent. After downing some soup and chips, Daniel and I set off in the steady rain into the dark.

The idea of running in chilly rain is never appealing, but once we got going, it wasn't so bad. The first 3 or 4 miles out of there were uphill, but I felt okay as we settled into a steady hike pace. It was great having some good company, and Daniel had the bright idea to put some soup in a zip lock bag and carry that for me. So that way I had access to soup in the long hours between aid stations. About every thirty to forty-five minutes, I'd drink some soup from the zip lock and munch on some chips that we also carried along. That strategy worked wonders on maintaining my energy levels!

We stopped for refueling at the next aid station at mile 68 and then hit more uphill, slowly moving up another mountain. The rain continued, and I kept having to add more layers as the temperature continued to drop in the low forties. Every now and then, we'd see other runners, and I remember seeing a lot of them struggling to stay upright as the amount of mud on the course increased. I was still feeling well physically, but the thickening mud definitely slowed the paces down a bit.

When we were several miles out from Beaver Lodge, the next aid at mile 75, the rain started getting harder and something inside me just sparked. We were now descending or on flatter sections, so I picked up the pace to a strong run and held that for several miles. Daniel was still with me of course, but it was a kind of "nose to the grindstone" moment when we didn't talk for a while and just focused on covering ground efficiently. Before we knew it, a gradually lightening sky indicated the first signs of daylight, and we rolled up to Beaver Lodge. The really awesome thing here was that my brother-in-law, Dillon, greeted us as we ran up! I knew that he was planning on arriving at some point to cheer me on and help crew, but I thought he might be showing up as early as mile 61, so it was a big relief to see him at Beaver Lodge!

***

Mom's note: Steven's blog comments end here, but his Bear YouTube video tells his whole story.

My Perspective on "the Bear"

In September 2014, Steven ran his first 100-mile race. It began in Utah, wound through trails and mountain paths around Bear Lake, and ended in Idaho. The race had epic weather changes from the beginning at sixty-five degrees to mile 25 where it spiked to ninety degrees. Then through the night, a storm front came through with freezing rain and wind, creating very muddy conditions on the trails.

This was the only one of Steven's 100 milers that Jay and I weren't a part of because I was still working full time at the hospital laboratory in Rome, Georgia. I had to work that specific weekend in September and tried to keep informed on Steven's progress by checking the Bear website. After nightfall, around mile 50 for Steven, there was little or no communication or updates on the site because the storm front and bad weather conditions prevented cell phone reception, and the race directors had only limited two-way radio lines open. (We became aware that most of these long races in remote locations do have limited communication.)

Our daughter's husband, Dillon, was out on the West Coast for a meeting and decided to fly to Idaho to help be a part of Steven's backup crew. He rented a car at the airport and used his phone GPS to find Steven's current location—until it stopped working. He literally found his way to the aid station at Beaver Lodge "on a wing and a prayer." Dillon followed a dirt road and, when he saw people outside a lodge, he asked, "Is this lodge where the Bear Lake race runners come through?"

They told him, "Yes, it is."

He parked and went inside.

It was the mile 75 aid station. When Steven and Daniel got there, Dillon was able to meet them outside. Then they went inside to eat food and take a break.

What a wonderful reunion!

Dillon was then able to communicate with his wife Amy, our daughter, and tell her that Steven was eating soup and feeling better. (He'd gotten really sick on the course when the temperatures had soared to around ninety degrees.) Amy called me and told me that he was doing better, and we both cried happy tears. Then when Dillon texted us a picture of Steven eating a pancake at mile 85, we knew he was going to be able to finish the race!

Dillon sent more videos and pictures, many of which are included in Steven's Bear YouTube video.

After the finish, the crew and runners went to eat since they were so hungry.

Steven says that any runner can burn 100 or more calories per mile during these races. Even though they ingest food, energy gels, and water, it's not enough to compensate for the total calories they burn (between 10,000 and 16,000).

The crew stayed at Eric and Shannon's house in Idaho, so they all slept well that night.

The next day was Sunday, and I was at the hospital working when I got a call from Steven. It was so good to hear his voice! He had just woken up and was sleeping downstairs at Eric's house in the dark, but he was alive and well. I told him he was my hero, and I was so happy that he had finished the race and was okay! He said he was still really tired but so glad he could rest now.

I give all the glory to God and thank him for sending angels in the form of Steven's friends and brother-in-law, who helped him through it!

CHAPTER 4

What it would take to Qualify for the UTMB

I t seems unlikely, to me, that many people who are runners would want to run in 100-mile races. And it seems even more unlikely that they would want to compete in France in the UTMB (Ultra- Trail du Mont-Blanc), where the runners race through three different countries—France, Switzerland, and Italy—up, down, and around the Alps, specifically Mt. Blanc. But they do! In fact, so many apply that the race is limited to approximately 2,400 runners.

Not only that, but these runners have to qualify to apply by running a combination of specific races (100-milers and 50-milers) that are on the approved list of the race committee. This list directed most of Steven's race choices for the three years that followed his decision to pursue UTMB qualification.

After Steven completed the Bear 100 in 2014, he was on the road to qualify for the UTMB in Chamonix, France! Once that got into his head, it became a goal and a dream!

Since his life verse is Philippians 4:13, "I can do all things through Christ who strengthens me" (NKJV), he would not be doing this alone. God would be with him all the way!

The following chapters are comprised of details from blogs, posts, and journals about the many races it would take to qualify and then compete in the UTMB in 2018.

Also included is a massive plan that Steven implemented to totally change his nutrition and way of life through a Whole30 diet.

Oh, and by the way, Steven would also buy and renovate two houses during this process, one in Nashville, Tennessee, and one in La Pine, Oregon. I've always told him that he's the most resourceful person I've ever known—for example, no amount of time or energy or materials are ever wasted. So much of his runner's story is intertwined with his renovation story, as is life!

What seems impossible to us isn't, as, "With God all things are possible" (Matthew 19:26) NKJV

CHAPTER 5

The Road to Bryce Canyon, Part I

I went into the Oak Mountain 50K in Birmingham, Alabama, with high hopes, fresh legs, and perfect weather (thirty-five to fifty-five degrees and sunny) on March

28, 2015. Leading up to the race, I had seen some of my best training ever, with high miles and solid speed work throughout January, February, and the first part of March. I try to set three goals for my ultras, which I call A, B, and C goals. A is maybe impossible, but with perfect conditions and perfect racing, it's within the realm. B is a solid goal that will still be hard to reach, but I know there's a decent shot at it. C is acceptable—not the best performance but I can live with it. So going into Oak Mountain, here they were: A—sub 5 hours, B—5:30, C—6:00. I also had Scott Thompson and Ryne Anderson racing with me from our RunWILD training group. So it was really cool to be down there with some buddies with similar abilities and goals.

We roll up to the race start in plenty of time, but as race start time of 7:30 a.m. approaches, we are doing last-minute warm-ups and gear/fuel checking. When 7:29 a.m. comes, I say, "We should probably get over to the start line since they said the race would start at 7:30 *sharp*."

Sure enough, as we are walking over, the race director very officially says to all participants, "You guys should probably get moving." And that was his version of the start gun!

After a quick half mile of road, we hit the yellow trail, which immediately had some steep climbs and descents, very similar to Percy Warner trails in Nashville. I kept my effort strong, wanting to keep my position at that point and at least start on track for a sub-five-hour race. About a mile or so in, Ali Edwards, the leading female runner from Birmingham, passed me with a "nice job" comment, and I settled in behind her for a while. We chatted some. When she said her name, I remembered that she had won Lookout

Mountain 50-miler a few years ago, so I knew I was in fast/good company. I ended up running and talking with her and another guy named Jeff from Franklin, Tennessee, all the way to the first aid station at about mile 7, which we hit in 1:08. My sub-five-hour pace goal for that distance was one hour, ten minutes.

Ali and Jeff stopped to refuel, but my plan was to move on through that first aid and not stop until the next one at mile 14.7. I pulled ahead on my own, feeling really strong. The next 7 miles really pushed the pace, and I was in a euphoric state, which derived from perfect temperatures, beautiful trails, and just feeling solid physically. As I neared the second aid station several minutes ahead of my top goal pace, the course markings weren't clear to me, and I ended up going off course and partway up a steep rocky embankment that definitely wasn't right. I said a few silent curses to myself for blowing the bank of extra minutes I had worked so hard to shave off but still arrived at Peavine Falls aid station on "A"-goal pace, precisely to the minute—2:19.

The Peavine station was a party complete with dance music, but I didn't linger for more than a minute or so until I was off on the White trail. This trail was absolutely gorgeous but extremely technical. There were super steep rocky descents that you really had to pick your way down carefully. It also seemed longer than it should have been, and I was trying my best to maintain pace and had been solo with no passes for a long time. I should mention that 50K should be 31 miles, but this race said it was 33 miles (Alabama math), and I definitely felt like a little of the bonus came in this section. I had hoped to arrive at the next aid at mile 21 in 3 hours and a few minutes but came in behind at

3:26, with legs that were finally starting to feel the efforts of the day. Fortunately, my parents were there with big smiles, and that was my first time seeing them for the day!

After taking a few minutes at mile 21 aid, the next several miles were uphill on the Red trail, a rocky fire road. This was when things gradually started crumbling. My legs were really starting to feel tired on that uphill. I jogged sections but felt like I was moving through molasses. My foot found a rock, and I tumbled on one of the few downhills. My stomach was nagging me also. Then I got a rock in my shoe that forced me to take my shoe off to remove it. I finally reached the top of the ridge and was able to run some flats at a more normal-ish pace. How had no one passed me yet?

After a stretch of a mile or so on the ridgetop, the route moved onto the White trail again. Although it was flat at this point, there were jutted rocks everywhere, and I found it impossible to get into a rhythm. I could feel Ultra signup pulling me back. "You're not supposed to be running the race this fast," it was saying. "Your ranking is too low for this; don't mess with the system!"

Sadly, I had to yield to its obnoxious siren call, since I felt the first signs of a leg cramp with a twitch in my left quad around mile 25. Ali passed me soon after with a "good job bro," along with another dude right behind her.

I finally made it into the next aid station, the "party" aid station at Peavine Falls at mile 26.(As in many ultramarathons, this aid station was used again at a further stage in the race for runners to eat, drink and fortify themselves for the next miles to run. A return to the same aid stations at different stages of the race is common to ultramarathons because of the length in miles (usually greater than 30 miles) and the size of the parks used for these races). A super helpful volunteer greeted me at this station. After shoveling some food down and also drink, I forced my hurting legs to jog down about a half-mile road stretch until I hit Red trail again. I had seen my friend Ryne catch up as I was leaving Peavine, and I saw him gaining as I turned onto the Red trail. Something kicked in, and I found another gear on some rolling and slightly technical downhill. I started pushing really hard. As a Nashville runner friend Phil Zimmerman says, "We may be friends, but if we are in a race, we are racing." I certainly wasn't moving as fast as in the beginning of the race, but I was pushing my body as much as I could physically and mentally handle to stay ahead of Ryne and another guy I had seen with him. Finally about a mile or two from the finish, my body said "enough," and I got sick multiple times in a row on the side of the trail. I got right back to running, but it was a slow slog to the finish. I finally made it there, with a thirteenth place finish (my best in an ultra), in five hours, forty-four minutes. Not my A or B goal, but I gave it my all and was so happy to be done! And the really awesome thing was that Ryne finished right after me at 5:46, and Scott finished in 5:55. So proud of my friends for awesome races!

And that's not the end of the story yet. After sitting down for a few minutes, I stood up only to have my legs start hurting. I don't mean I was sore; I mean my legs were screaming! I tried to walk it off, but I felt absolutely terrible and had no choice but to lie down on the ground beside the finish pavilion. Several people asked if I needed help, but I told them I was okay and that my parents were right there.

And then a beautiful blond girl, appearing to be in her

twenties, just starts doing things to help me. She props up my feet and has my parents bring me blankets from their car to keep me warm. I learn that her name is Britt and that she has run in the Boston Marathon three times. Am I in heaven? Nope, nope, it's real. And she is friends with Ali, who finished at 5:27 as the first female and came over and talked to me and Britt. Oh, did I mention that Britt is an ER physician? Maybe I stayed on the ground longer than I really needed to; maybe I didn't. Whatever the case, I started feeling better, and that was a great ending to a great race! Ultramarathons, I love you. You always challenge me, but you always leave me with some incredible memories!

***

Author's note: Angels always seem to show themselves when needed. Steven was severely dehydrated from being sick alongside the trail but recovered with her help and drinking fluids and eating salty chips! Thank you, Lord, for sending help at the right time!

He promises, "I will never leave you or forsake you" (Hebrews 13:5).

CHAPTER 6

The Road to Bryce Canyon, Part II

Cheating on Trails with a Road Race by Steven McNeal
April 26, 2015

About a week and a half before Nashville's biggest road race, the Country Music Marathon and half marathon, Wade Oliver (superfast road dude) comes into Nashville Running Company (the store where I was working at the time) and we both talk about how we are not signed up for the race. But every year that we don't do it, we end up wishing we were running when race day comes. Not wanting to have that regret again, I pulled the trigger and signed up for the half marathon, even though that wasn't necessarily the best choice for my Bryce 100 trail training. I knew it would set me back a little in terms of miles for the week of CMM and might cause me to need some extra recovery time after the race too. But since I had planned on the Tom King half in March and that got iced out and turned into a 5K, I really wanted to race a half and see what I could do.

My good friend Nash Harris kindly offered to help pace me in the CMM half as soon as he heard that I was signing up and gunning for my first sub-1:30. Nash is an awesome runner and an even more awesome dude in general, so I was stoked to get to race together. We came up with a race strategy, which mainly consisted of staying about ten seconds per mile under pace on flat and downhill sections to make up for the time we would lose on the uphills.

Race morning arrived with temps in the low sixties and high humidity. Rain was in the forecast and had caused much panic and stress among many, many folks, as you learn when you work in a running store. You get 50 million phone calls and questions about what in the world to do if, God forbid, it rains when you run. I personally was praying for rain to keep it cool, but the masses got their wish, and not a drop of rain fell during the race. Anyhoo, Nash and I found each other before the start, and we joined our friend Drew, who had similar goals for the race.

I've ran Country Music before, but it has been a few years, and I have gotten a bit faster. So this year, I had the luxury to be in Corral Numero Uno. It was a little surreal being in the front of thirty thousand people, so I tried to soak in the moment. The start gun finally went off, and we were moving. Even in Corral 1, people go out faster than they are capable of maintaining and they slow down. And there are still quite a large number of people per corral. So Nash, Drew, and I still had to weave our way through some folks, in addition to the general winding-ness of the first mile or two due to all of the turns. We were moving fast, but it took a good 2 miles or so until it felt like we had some breathing room and were able to settle into more of a rhythm.

In spite of the starting chaos and the long gradual uphill of Demonbreun Street, we arrived at the 5K mark a little ahead of schedule. I think all three of us felt like we were working, but we also knew that the initial miles of the race were some of the most difficult. Nash had talked to me before the race about walking through some of the water stops. So we actually did that a few times and stayed on pace. The humidity wasn't bothering me as much as I had thought it might, but it still helped to dump some cool water on my head at each water stop every mile or so.

We passed the 10K point still slightly ahead of schedule,

knowing that the 12th South hill lay just ahead. Going up 12th South, Drew pulled ahead. I could tell that Nash wasn't feeling great, and he started walking and then told me to go on. I definitely had no desire to leave him. But I could sense he didn't want me to wait, so I went on. I looked back a few times to see if he would catch up, but he was falling further behind. So I knew it was solo time. (Later he would catch up and finish the race just a few minutes behind me. He is a trooper.)

Once on my own, I was getting to the section of the course that is mostly flat or downhill, from miles 7 through 11ish. I felt really strong and was cruising a bit under goal pace (6:52/mile) and seeing a lot of 6:20 to 6:30 paces on the Garmin. I also saw a lot of friends and my parents spectating on the course, so that was always a boost to how I felt and probably to my pace too.

Thankfully, my energy held up well during the final 5K, even though it was starting to get more uncomfortable. I knew I was going to come in under goal pace. But about a quarter of a mile from the finish, I couldn't help the thought that it was just like doing a hard 400 yards on the track. So with a downhill and a resolve to make it hurt for that last push, I turned up to top speed and flew down that hill and then turned the corner and crossed the finish with a chip time of 1:28:02. Goal shattered, and it was a five-minute PR (personal record)! Then the really cool thing was seeing friends after the race and celebrating together—Drew had torched the course after pulling ahead of Nash and me and finished in 1:25!

I caught up with several other friends in the finish area, which was awesome. Then I started to jog back to NRC East, where I had parked to avoid traffic and get in some extra miles, when, lo and behold, I saw two people running in the distance who obviously didn't belong. I could tell from their form and stature that it was Phil Zimmerman and Beth Meadows, trail friends of mine, running around Tennessee Titans stadium. As it turned out, they were looking for me! The three of us ran back to NRC together and then handed out water to marathon runners.

So do I feel bad about cheating on the trails by doing a road race? Nah, I got in 17 miles total and some solid speedwork and had a blast with friends. Besides that, me and my crazy self got up early the day after the race and met up with my good friend Jeff Davis to run 20 miles at an out-of-town trail that was new to both of us. Yep, 20 miles the day after racing! I won't say it didn't hurt. But with a little sacrifice on my part, training for the Bryce 100 and the trails didn't suffer too much with my one-day fling.

***

Author's note: Jay and I saw Steven at mile 6 and then mile 10. Then we drove to NRC and parked our car to wait for him at the finish. While waiting, we started to help pass out cups of water to the runners continuing to run the marathon course. It was so fun holding out a cup in each hand and seeing multiple people grab a cup, drink it, and then continue running on toward the end. They would come in waves and most always said, "Thank you." Khette was there helping and said, "Thanks, Mom," after we finished. It's such a welcoming community at NRC. So good!

CHAPTER 7

The Road to Bryce Canyon, Part III

Frozen Head by Steven McNeal
May 18,2015

It's getting down to the wire with training for my biggest race of the year in less than three weeks, the Bryce Canyon 100 mile in Bryce Canyon, Utah. As I wrote about in my last post, I decided spur-of-the-moment style to run Country Music Half in Nashville a few weeks ago. That would have been fine to do if I hadn't also felt that, in order to do so, I needed to run 20 miles on trails the day after Country Music. I had fun (except for the hurting legs) on a new trail that day, but it really destroyed my legs and resulted in some seriously slow recovery. That next week, I only ran 7 miles total and felt bad doing it.

I had originally planned on two 80-mile weeks in a row after taking a recovery week post-CMM. That would be my last round of heavy training for Bryce before tapering. The first of those weeks I struggled to hit 60 miles total, but I did finish out the week with a 20-mile run with some friends at Bearwaller Gap on a day with record high temperatures. That. Hurt. If you haven't heard about or experienced the Bearwaller, just know that it has some memorable views and even more memorable hills.

I started the week after Bearwaller slowly since that run took it out of me. I just didn't have the energy for most of the week to do anything but easy runs. Knowing that I was missing the mark on my last week of training for Bryce, I began feeling underprepared. My training needed a last resort jump-start. Frozen Head—as in Frozen Head State Park, where a "little" race called the Barkley is run. The Barkley is considered by some to be the most difficult trail race in existence. If I could finish my last heavy week with a beefy run out there, I would feel much more at ease about where I stood with training overall, even if I again hit less than 80 miles for the week. If you even utter "Bearwaller" and "Frozen Head" within the same conversation, your game has been elevated. So, if I could run decent mileage at those trails on consecutive weekends, I'd be set.

When Jeff Davis tells you that your miles will be slower on certain trails, you know that it's true. So, after he told me about Frozen Head and gave me some insight on the trails there, I knew I had a full day ahead of me and left Nashville bright and early at 5:30 a.m. Three hours and a coffee and restroom stop later, I arrived at the park.

Once on trails at Frozen Head, one quickly realizes that you are in a very rugged but very lush place. In the first two miles, I gained about 900 feet of elevation, which was made a little easier on beautiful narrow single-track trails with great views.

I also noticed some interesting new wildlife, like some bright red lizards that I saw dozens of on the trails and crazy little mini-lobster-looking things that I suppose were crawdads and hissed at me when I got close. Eventually, I got to the ridgetop and was rewarded with some cool fog rolling across the quiet trail that snaked along the spine of the ridge. I made my way to the fire tower, positioned atop a 3,300-foot peak that normally allows for views of the surrounding valleys and even the Smokies. However, my view was totally fogged in.

Oh well. It was a nice spot to plop down for a quick lunch. After that, I spent several hours going up and down fire roads, which were wide and rocky but not too scenic. My energy levels stayed strong throughout the miles, and I had zero stomach issues. Several people have recently recommended ginger to help with nausea and digestion problems on my longer runs, so I tried ginger chews from Whole Foods for the first time on this run and didn't have any issues. So, whether they actually helped or not, I will keep using them.

Towards the end of my run, I made my way down a different trail that followed a stream and led to a small waterfall and a rock cave called Panther Rock House. Pretty cool! Since things were jiving physically and I had covered ground steadily for most of the day, I wrapped up the day at Frozen Head with 30 miles total in under eight hours, including 6,600 plus feet of gain. Not too shabby for a day's work.

And now the countdown begins to Bryce 100, just two and a half weeks away!

CHAPTER 8

Bryce Canyon 100

Jay and I went to church on Sunday morning, May 31, 2015, and were a part of a great worship service where the choir sang "Indescribable" and "Untitled Hymn." Then the youth praise team sang "I Am a Friend of God" and "You Are Awesome in this Place, Mighty God." Then a special hymn was sung called "Broken and Spilled Out." These songs would play in my head several times on our way out west to Utah and during Steven's Bryce Canyon 100-mile race. In the afternoon, we drove to Nashville and stayed at Steven's condo for the night. We got up at 3:00 a.m. the next morning and left toward our next stop in Independence, Missouri, for the night.

On the way, around lunchtime, we saw a sign that said "Joe's Barbeque." It reminded us of our friend Joe, who also happens to be a truck driver. I sent him a text with the picture of the sign, and in less than twenty minutes Joe texted us and said, "Where are you guys?"

After we told him, Joe said, "I'm only about fifteen minutes from where you are. Why don't we meet for lunch?"

So it was a date! So fun catching up with him.

In the meantime, Steven and his friend Casey had begun their drive from Nashville in Casey's Lexus. Casey had accepted a new position as a nurse manager at Cedars Sinai Medical Center in Los Angeles, and she was going to crew for Steven at the Bryce 100 and then drive on to LA. We were to pick up Daniel, another of Steven's good friends, who would also crew and pace for him at Bryce, in Denver in a couple of days. Steven and Casey would drive to Manhattan, Kansas, to stay with a friend's parents who live there.

Our next motel stop would be Colby, Kansas, just near the border of Colorado. But first we drove through Kansas and noticed that there was a sign pointing to the Eisenhower Presidential Library and Memorial in Abilene, Kansas. Dwight Eisenhower was president of the United States when I was born, so I was really interested and wanted to stop and see the memorial.

It was beautiful there. Around a fountain outside and a long rectangular sidewalk with grass in the middle, many people were walking their children and babies in strollers and just enjoying the day. It seemed like a college campus. We went inside and saw a black-and-white movie about Eisenhower's life. He was born into a family and had five brothers. He was also a general in World War II and commander of the Allied Forces. He made the decision to send our troops in the D-Day invasion, a turning point of the war.

As we left there and went to our hotel for the night, we

saw many windmills, which are used for electrical power along the sides of the road. It was June 2, and I remembered that it was Amy and Dillon's fourteenth wedding anniversary, so we got a card and mailed it from Kansas.

On June 3, Wednesday, we got up early and left, going west on I-70 toward Colorado. We were supposed to pick up Daniel in Denver around noon. Steven and Casey had already gotten him from the Denver Airport on Tuesday after they had unloaded most of their luggage at their friend Joel's house in Denver. Casey had a basically two-seat white Lexus, but a person could sit in the back if all other luggage was removed. Steven, Casey, and Daniel had a great time in Denver together. They cooked dinner and went on a five-mile hike in the evening. They took a beautiful picture of them at sunset with the Denver skyline in the background.

They brought Daniel to Union Station the next day, where he would wait for us to pick him up. After we picked him up, we drove on through I-70 and up the mountains west of Denver. For lunch we ate at Smokin' Joes Barbeque, where we ordered our food and took it outside to tables there. We saw several people on rafts going down a mountain river. It was so fun to be outside and see the beautiful views of Colorado!

The next day, we headed to Utah. Steven and Casey were already there. Steven texted that they had spent the night in a teepee near a campsite and the temperature that morning had been 29 degrees—brrr.They had a cabin for the next night, thank goodness. We pulled up to Foster's Motel near Bryce Canyon about 1:30 p.m. As we were walking over to the market next door to our hotel, we heard a car horn honking, and it was Steven and Casey driving into the parking lot!

They hugged us and then said they were hungry from hiking, so we went to Ruby's Inn downtown and had a good dinner.

Steven had rented a small cabin for the night so that they could be warm and sleep well the night before the race. It was so cute, with a small front porch and two bunk beds inside. After we got them settled, there was a prerace meeting for runners and crew outside the Rubys Inn. We all went over to the area and met some really nice people.

Steven went to the preregistration tent and got his number for the race, 413. (I said it was 13 for my birthday and 4 for the number of people in his crew.) He also got a Bryce Canyon T-shirt and a 100-mile sticker for his car (that he still has on the Honda Civic in our garage). I bought my grandsons, Zach and Matthew, each a T-shirt just like Steven's. After hearing the race instructions at the meeting, the runners and crew went to another tent, where pizza and toppings were provided for them.

Daniel told Jay and me that the best place for us to meet him and Casey in the morning was the Proctor aid station at mile 21 around 10:00 a.m. We hugged Steven goodbye since we wouldn't see him until mile 21 the next day, said bye to Daniel and Casey, and went back to Fosters Motel to get some sleep ourselves. Tomorrow was race day!

On June 5, 2015, the Bryce Canyon start day began around 5:00 a.m. with us up and getting ready. I had been praying off and on all night and had just seen a friend post a Bible verse that was really relevant to Steven's race.

Isaiah 46:4 reads, "I have made you and I will carry you, I will sustain you and I will rescue you" (NIV).

I texted that verse to Steven and Godspeed and good luck with his race—and that I loved him. He was at the race start and texted me back. "Thanks, Mom. I love you too." There's something surreal about sitting in a dark hotel room before sunrise and knowing your son is going to begin a 100-mile journey through trails, cliffs, and mountains in Utah only a few miles away.

Since we were ready to go, we went across the parking lot to Foster's, a cafe/restaurant, and ordered breakfast—French toast for me and the Foster's special plate for Jay. It was great! Then we drove over to the little cabin to pick up Daniel and Casey and take them to the first aid station where we were to meet Steven at Proctors Lake, Utah. When we got to the gravel road near the dirt trail to Proctor, we parked on the side of the road behind twenty cars that were already parked there. We saw a line of people who were waiting on ATVs to take them up the dirt trail to the aid station. After ten minutes of waiting and finding out that it was about a fifteen-minute ride to the aid, Daniel and Casey said they would hike the 3 miles to the aid station. We would wait on the ATVs and then ride there.

It took nearly an hour before it was our turn to ride there. Jay rode on the green John Deere ATV, and I rode on the red one. It was a harrowing ride over rocks and trails that looked down the side of a mountain. I was hanging on for dear life! The lady who drove my red ATV was evidently a legend in ultrarunning. She had run a 135-mile course years before. She drove the ATV like a woman possessed. When I finally got out of the vehicle at Proctor, I felt like every bone in my body had been jolted around. And Jay said he felt like he had been a part of an action scene in a James Bond movie.

When we walked up the hill to Proctor aid, we immediately saw Daniel and Casey in a line of people waiting to get a ride back to where the cars were parked. Daniel said, "We missed seeing Steven at this aid station by five minutes"—according to the crew who keep a record of all runners by their race number and name.

At every aid station, there were workers/volunteers who helped give runners food, water, and/or Gatorade, even if their crews couldn't make it there. One of the workers had a clipboard and wrote down the race number of each runner coming through and his or her time so far. So, after I took a picture of the beautiful view, we got in line to go back to our car. We all got in a gray SUV and traveled back down the mountain.

After getting back to our car, we were starving, since we hadn't had anything to eat in several hours. So when we saw the Galaxy Diner a few miles away, we went there to eat. The owner's name was Hatch, and he said he'd built the diner and renovated it himself. The diner was decorated with pictures of movie stars from the past, like Lucille Ball and Elvis. It had airplane propeller fans on the ceiling too. The breakfast plates were huge, and the food was really good.

Daniel calculated that we had forty-five minutes to get to the next aid station at mile 41 in time to meet Steven. So we followed his GPS coordinates to Straight Canyon aid. There were already about forty people there waiting when we drove up. So Jay and I got out, and Daniel and Casey drove up a hill to park the Jeep. Then they brought us two camp chairs from the car so we could sit and wait on

Steven. How nice! While we were waiting, Scott Bell, one of Steven's friends, came over to us and introduced himself and his wife, Mary. It was so nice to talk to them and meet their three boys too.

After an hour of waiting, Jay and I decided to walk up a hill along the path of runners coming through the aid station. While on the hill, we met a nice Irish lady and her husband, who were waiting on their daughter. She was from Oregon and running in her first 100-mile race. After their daughter came through, we met a man from San Francisco who was going to pace another runner later. He told us he'd run in the Western States 100-mile years before. It had snowed in the Squaw Valley portion of Western States that year.

Then the weather went crazy. Thunder boomed and lightning struck. So we gave our umbrella to Daniel and Casey and walked to our car. We drove closer to the aid station, and then it began to hail. Casey took a picture of the hail covering her camp chair. Then it stopped hailing, and we saw Steven running down the hill to the aid station, at 5:20 p.m.—mile 41. Yay!

Steven sat on a pile of logs near the aid tent while Daniel and Casey got him food and water. After he began running again, the rest of us got some food at Foster's and then drove to the Crawford aid station at mile 51. There was a campfire, a tent, and an outdoor enclosed bathroom—how wonderful. We got our camp chairs and sat around the fire and waited for runners to come through. One of the runners was an older man named Bobby, who was sixty-six years old. He looked like Santa Claus. His wife had heated macaroni and cheese over the campfire in a pot. Bobby sat down next to his wife and ate the mac and cheese out of the pot. His wife told us she'd been with him for all seventy-five of his 100-mile runs and that this race was his seventy-sixth! He had run seven 100-milers this year alone, and Bryce was his 8th. He'd retired from his job this year and was trying to complete one hundred 100-milers in his lifetime. We saw Bobby at the finish. He told us he'd had to drop out of this race but was still working directing cars where to park in the parking area.

Back at mile 51 aid, we had waited for about an hour, and it was beginning to get dark outside. So I walked to the cattle gate fence near the trail where runners were coming up a hill from the famous pink cliffs area of the canyon. I was praying that Steven would get there before it was totally dark. I looked down at the ground and saw some money folded up and lying on the grass. I picked it up and asked the people standing there if it belonged to them. They said, "No. It belongs to you now." It turned out to be seven dollars, and I hoped that was a good sign that Steven would be coming soon.

Sure enough, in the next few minutes, here he came running up the hill at 9:30 p.m. I called out to him and told him that I had some bread and some Gatorade. He said he'd been thinking about real Gatorade. It was like music to my ears because I knew he was having trouble retaining enough food and electrolytes. He drank about half of the bottle of Gatorade. Daniel told him he had a club sandwich for him, and Steven was able to eat some of that too. Then Daniel refilled Steven's water vest and put Gatorade in his extra bottle. He also got potato chips to put in a sandwich bag for him. Casey asked Steven if he needed his headlamp, since it was getting dark.

He said, "Oh yeah," and got it out of his pack and put it on his head. Then he asked when he would see us again.

Daniel had estimated that we could be at Proctor aid at mile 81at 6:00 a.m., but he felt like jumping in and pacing Steven right then. Steven said we should probably go back to the hotel and get some rest, so we said goodbye and drove to our motel.

When I lie down to go to sleep that night I thought, "Steven is still running, and there's lightning outside. If it were up to me, Lord, I would go and pull him off that trail right now."

But the Lord had other plans. So I prayed for protection and safety and strength for my son's journey.

At that point, Casey and Daniel had already turned in the keys to their cabin, since they could only have it for one night. They didn't have a room because every hotel in the area was full. We told them that our room had carpet on the floor; they could use their sleeping bags and sleep there. So they did.

Since Daniel was going to pace with Steven beginning at mile 81, we got up at 5:00 a.m. and got ready by 5:30 to go to Proctor aid station. It was sunrise.

We were hoping the race workers would be better prepared to take us to Proctor than they had been yesterday, and they were. Two of the ATV drivers were adding gas to their vehicles and told us they would be ready to take us in a few minutes. Jay got on the green ATV, and Daniel, Casey, and I got on the red one. Our driver was named Dusty, and he was a pilot from Peachtree City, Georgia. His family was from Utah and had called him and asked if he could help with the race crew. He had driven from Georgia and had also brought his boat so he could have fun with his family the next weekend and during the summer.

It took us fifteen minutes to get to Proctor aid. When we got there, we walked up the hill toward the aid tent and saw ten people already there. Some of the guys had built a fire in a metal barrel that had four legs and the number *100* carved out of one of the sides (for the Bryce 100).The outside temperature was 37 degrees that morning, so we had all dressed in layers to keep warm. Casey had brought her sleeping bag, so she covered up with that. Jay and I stayed near the fire. We could see the trail really well from that location, so we kept our place there for about two hours.

We had seen several runners come through this part of the trail. Then I saw a runner about a mile away wearing a black T-shirt and black shorts. I thought, *That looks like Steven.* But I walked hurriedly down the hill so I could get a closer look. I called out his name, and he raised his arm in greeting. Yes, it was him!

Our ATV driver, Dusty, was there at the bottom of the hill and said to me, "Is that your runner?"

I said, "It sure is, and he's my son."

Dusty had the biggest smile.

When Steven got close to me, I told him that Daniel was up near the aid tent and was waiting for him, since he would be pacing him until the race finish. Casey walked with Steven up the hill, and then she and Daniel helped get water and food for him. Jay and I went inside the tent so we could help too. Steven asked me to fill up his spare water bottle with half Gatorade and half Coke, so I did. He also wanted to eat pancakes, so I got those and also put two extra pancakes in a sandwich bag and put them in his vest. After that and since he had sat in a camp chair for a few minutes, he said he was ready to continue on. Daniel was waiting for him outside and Steven saw him and said, "Let's go!" So off they went on the last 19 miles of the race. I knew that Steven would be okay now that he had Daniel with him.

When Casey, Jay, and I got to the bottom of the hill past the aid tent, there was Dusty, our ATV driver, with a big smile and saying, "Are you ready to go?" He had waited for us the whole time! We got into his ATV and rode the three miles back to our car feeling really good about Steven being able to finish. It was a great experience so far.

Then we drove a couple of miles to the Galaxy Diner for breakfast. Hatch, the owner, was there and told us that he was glad we came back to eat there again. He told us the guy who had finished first in the Bryce Canyon 100 had just eaten breakfast there that morning.

Casey told us about her plans for driving to LA the next day and that it should take her eight hours to get to her new apartment in Beverly Hills. She said the movers were bringing her furniture on Monday. Since we had some free time after breakfast and before we needed to be at the finish line in order to see Steven and Daniel, we asked Casey if she wanted us to take her to her car. She said yes and that she also wanted to do some souvenir shopping at Ruby's Inn. So that's what we did.

We dropped her off at her car and told her we would be back for her in an hour. I had seen a vacancy sign on a hotel across the street at a new Best Western Plus, so I asked Jay if we could go over there and get a nice room for Casey,

Daniel, and Steven for the night. That way, they could have a relaxing night after the race and a nice breakfast buffet the next morning because Casey had to leave by 6:00 a.m. The hotel had a beautiful rustic lobby with a huge fireplace and massive couches and a rocking chair.

After we got the room keys, Jay and I went outside to our black Jeep, which now looked brown since we had driven through so many muddy roads. We saw a Sinclair gas station, the one with the green dinosaur logo, with a carwash. So we got some gas and paid for a carwash. While we were getting gas, a lady came up to us and said, "I think you need to get your car washed." We told her that we were going to get that done in a few minutes. Then she asked us where we were from, and we said, "Georgia." She said she was from California and she didn't have an accent like we did. Ha ha! What a comedian. Then it was time to pick up Casey so that we could go to the finish.

We drove a few miles past Foster's motel and followed the GPS to the race finish area. I recognized several of the runners there from seeing them come through Proctor at mile 81 when we were waiting on Steven that morning. Also we saw Bobby, the sixty-six-year-old runner we had seen at mile 51. He was directing cars about where to park. His knees had given out around mile 70, and he had to drop out this time. But he seemed cheerful and gave us a smile when we passed him.

Casey and I sat on a log near the finish line so that we could see Steven and Daniel come through. It started to rain again just about the time we saw them running at the top of the final hill. It was about 2:45 p.m. They ran down the hill, and Daniel ran to the right since he was pacing.

Steven came across the finish line with a time of thirty-two hours forty minutes! I was taking pictures and giving him a hug when a young lady said that she had taken a video of us at the finish. She was going to send it to Steven. That was really nice of her.

It was raining more now, so we all got in our Jeep. Daniel said that it was the first time we had all been together in the car for two days. It was a great feeling. Steven said all he wanted to do was to take a shower, so we drove to the Best Western Plus and walked through the lobby and up to their room. When we got to the room, Daniel said the room was even nicer than the rooms he stays in when he goes on business trips for his work. I'm so glad they liked it because they deserved a good place to stay after sleeping on the floor the previous night. And Steven was running all night, so he didn't get to sleep at all.

Steven took two showers, one to get the top coat of mud off and another just to get clean. His shoes were covered in mud, and he put them in a far corner on the floor of the bathroom and eventually threw them away. After they all got cleaned up and were ready to go, we went to Ruby's Inn. First we stopped at the main race tent, and Steven collected his Bryce 100 belt buckle for finishing the race. He also got a Bryce 100 T-shirt that he wore the next day. Then we drove over to the restaurant at Ruby's Inn where we had decided to eat because they had a great buffet. Steven ordered steak and mashed potatoes. We all had good meals and then ate ice cream from the buffet for dessert. The table next to us had four senior adults from China. They each had a card with the food they wanted to order, printed in English, so that they could give the card to the waiter. One of them would say something funny in Chinese, and then everyone at their table would laugh together just alike. It was cute! Steven paid for all of our dinners and said he wanted to do that for "his crew." It was so nice of him!

After dinner, we went to the main lobby of Ruby's Inn. There was a large stone fireplace, and we all sat down on the hearth in front of the fireplace. We asked a nice lady customer to take our picture there. Since we had our picture taken there two days before, we now had our "after race" photo. Everyone was tired and wanted to go back to the room, so we went back there. Casey would be leaving early in the morning for LA, so we said goodbye to her. Jay and I went back to our motel and slept really well that night.

The next morning, we got ready and went to Fosters restaurant for breakfast. After that, we checked out of the hotel and drove over to the Best Western where Steven and Daniel were staying. Steven had texted me earlier and said that the breakfast bar there was amazing! They had gotten up early and eaten with Casey before she left for Los Angeles, an eight-hour drive for her. She was going to her new apartment and then starting her new job at Cedars Sinai hospital the next week.

It was Sunday and was going to be a full day of celebration after Steven's 100-mile run. We drove on our way to the North Rim of the Grand Canyon in Arizona. We had been driving for several hours, and Daniel said that we were driving past the last place to eat lunch before we got to the entrance of the Grand Canyon. So I pulled into the parking lot of the Jacob's Lake Inn. We went inside and walked to the right past the gift shop and were seated at a table in the right corner of the restaurant. There were paintings and handmade rugs and other works of art on every wall. Beside our table was a portrait of a beautiful wild gray horse. Both Steven and I noticed it, and he took a picture of it. We ordered our lunch. And then, as we were waiting for our food, Steven said, "I think I'm going to buy that painting."

I said, "That will look really nice in your condo."

Steven said, "I don't really have a place for it. I'm going to give it to you."

Tears began streaming down my face, and I said, "It would look great on our fireplace mantle in our living room."

He said I could leave it for him in my will, and I said, "It's already yours, whenever you want it."

Steven made arrangements with the waitress to buy the portrait. She asked one of the ladies in the gift shop to help and wrap it in heavy plastic, since we thought we might have to tie it on top of our Jeep. But Steven and Daniel were able to fit the three-foot-by-three-foot portrait in the inside back of the Jeep.

When we were all getting into the car to head to the Grand Canyon, I realized that I hadn't given Steven a hug. So I got out of the Jeep and walked over to him and gave him a hug and told him, "Thank you so much. It's a wonderful gift."

About five minutes after we started on the last thirty miles to the Grand Canyon, it started to rain. So we were really glad that the picture fit in the back instead of on top. I still have the beautiful wild horse portrait above our mantle and see it every day!

When we got to the entrance gate of the Grand Canyon North Rim, a ranger took our thirty-dollar entrance fee and said that it was good for seven days in all parts of the Grand Canyon. We drove onto the parking lot near the main lodge. We walked into the lodge. There were several leather couches and chairs and massive windows looking out over the Grand Canyon with a view for miles. We walked outside on a porch to the right that had rocking chairs and a four-foot wall in front. Steven wanted Daniel to take a picture of him wearing his Bryce Canyon cap while he sat on the wall's ledge. Steven said he was secure because he was sitting down. But several people, including me, were holding our breaths the whole time until he got back onto the porch.

Next we decided to take a half-mile hike on a walking trail called Bridal Veil Trail. It was a three-foot wide path winding around to a ledge where you could see a closer view of the North Rim. It was a beautiful day and we had a twelve-year-old boy take our picture there—one of our favorite pictures of the whole trip!

After that, we walked back to the lodge and sat on one of the leather couches and enjoyed the view. Then we left the lodge and saw a faucet coming out of a rock with a sign that said fresh mountain spring water. So we filled up our water bottles there, and it tasted so good!

We decided to drive from the Grand Canyon to Flagstaff, Arizona, about 200 miles. Daniel had eaten at a burger place called El Diablo when he was in Flagstaff before, so we went to the downtown area and found the restaurant before the sun set. We were in a line to order our food and then went outside to eat at picnic tables, family style. At our table was a couple from Southampton, England, who were going to take a train ride to the Grand Canyon the next day. He worked at the boat docks helping senior citizens board ships there.

Little did we know that, three years later, we would board the *Queen Mary II* in Southampton. After we ate, we went to our hotel.

The next morning, we ate breakfast and then went back downtown to do some shopping before we left for Phoenix. One of the stores was Patagonia, where there was a large (four-foot-by-five-foot) photo on the wall behind the cashier's desk. The photo was of four wild horses taken in Patagonia, Argentina. I told the lady behind the desk about the portrait Steven had bought for me of the wild gray horse. She asked if we had seen the Belmont Stakes race on Saturday. We said no, because Steven was running in his 100-mile Bryce Canyon race. The lady said that the horse who'd won that race was American Pharoah, and that was his third first place finish in a row to make him the winner of the triple crown! This was the first triple crown winner in thirty-seven years. His jockey said that "he breathed different air" than the other horses. Horses are truly remarkable animals!

After visiting the Run Flagstaff running store, it was time to drive to Phoenix, since Steven and Daniel had a flight scheduled for 4:30, and it was 144 miles from Flagstaff to Phoenix. On the way to Phoenix, we stopped for lunch at Beni's Pizza in Black Canyon City, Arizona. The food was really good, and we even had some pizza left over that Daniel and Steven took with them to eat while waiting on the plane in Phoenix.

The elevation in Flagstaff is seven thousand feet, and Steven explained that the elevation in Phoenix is two thousand feet. So there is a five thousand-foot change in altitude going there. Since it was June 8, there would also be a rise in temperature. It went from 75 degrees in Flagstaff to 108 degrees in Phoenix. We found the Southwest terminal at the Phoenix airport and helped them unload their backpacks and luggage. We hugged them and told them to have a safe trip. They told us to have a safe trip too, since we would be driving back to Georgia in the next few days.

Jay and I drove about 186 miles to Holbrook, Arizona, to our hotel and arrived before sunset. Our room was on the second floor, and we stood outside and watched one of the most beautiful sunsets ever!

The next day, we drove to Santa Rosa, New Mexico, and exited I-40 to go to our hotel on Route 66, which parallels I-40 for hundreds of miles in the southwest. As usual, we asked at the desk for recommendations for restaurants and were directed to Joseph's about a mile down the road. The food was delicious, and the coconut cream pie was homemade and the best!

On Wednesday, we drove through the rest of New Mexico; the northern panhandle of Texas (which is Garth Brooks country as indicated by multiple signs); and on to El Reno, Oklahoma, where we checked into the local Best Western. The manager at the desk suggested Sid's Diner for dinner since it would be featured on the Food Network's Triple-D in a few weeks. We drove to the downtown area and parked at Sid's. We went inside and saw one table available so we sat there. All the food was cooked on a large grill behind the main counter. We had the best burgers we'd ever eaten and thin-sliced french fries cooked to perfection and then served on red-and-white-checked paper and placed in a basket. Their vanilla milkshake tasted like ones we used to have at the drugstore counter in the '60s when we were growing up. When we went up front to pay for our meal, we saw a large map of the United States on the wall. The owner, Marty (not Sid) asked us to put a thumbtack on our area of Georgia. He gave us a card and told us that this restaurant would be featured on TV next week. We thanked him for the great meal and then left to go back to our hotel for the night.

The next morning as we were eating breakfast, we saw that a cattle truck had overturned on I-40 east, and many cattle had escaped and were on the interstate.

We knew we were going to have some delays on our way to Oklahoma City and then on to Memphis. We were rerouted onto a parallel side road for several miles. Several hours later, we got a call from our friend, Joe, a truck driver. He asked, Were we in Oklahoma near him? We looked at the map and said yes and that we'd meet him for lunch. We had a fun time catching up with him and then went on our way to Memphis, Tennessee. At our hotel there, the guy at the desk suggested Marlowe's Barbeque, one of Elvis' favorite places. It was located near Graceland, Elvis's house, and the restaurant had a pink cadillac car ride service. We called for the pink cadillac and were driven there in style. The food was great, and the place had lots of Elvis memorabilia.

On the next day, Friday, June 12, 2015, we decided to go home using I-40 through Nashville instead of US-72 through Alabama. We texted Steven to see whether he was working at NRC East or West store. He said he would be at NRC East starting at 11:00 a.m. When we got to the store, we parked and went inside. We saw Jackson at the front desk, and he said hello to us. Then we saw Steven standing on the left side of the store, and he was smiling. We had brought the rest of our Krispy Kreme donuts from Memphis for the people working at the store.

Then Steven went outside to our car with us, and we gave him his running shoes and air mattress that we had brought back from Utah.

He had gotten a belt buckle from the Bryce 100 race, and he had worn it that day. When he showed it to us, I thought, *Less than a week ago, he ran 100 miles in Bryce Canyon, Utah*! He looked rested and said he felt good.

After we hugged him and told him we loved him, we said goodbye and drove to I-24 east toward home in Summerville, Georgia. When we got home at 3:30 pm, I checked our mileage; we had left home over ten days ago, and it turned out that we had driven 4,400 miles and been in fifteen states in twelve days. Thank you, Lord, for safe travels and a good race for Steven! He had completed one more step toward running in UTMB!

CHAPTER 9

The Road to UTMB, Chamonix, France, Part I

North Face Wisconsin 50-Miler Race Report by Steven McNeal
October 12, 2015

A few months ago, I signed up for this flatlander's race, as I was perusing the options to give me the final qualifying point I needed to get into another race I want to do in Europe next year. Ultra-Trail du Mont-Blanc, or UTMB for short, is a bucket-list race for a lot of people once they enter the ultra gateway, and I got the itch to try to get in after I realized I was close to qualifying by virtue of some of the longer ultras I had completed in the past two years. So I signed up for the North Face Challenge race in Wisconsin, as it is one of the few relatively nearby races that would give me my final point needed to enter the UTMB lottery come December 2015. Some bonuses of choosing NFCW would be that it is/was much flatter than most of the ultras I had done so far, and the likelihood of warm weather in Wisconsin in October was fairly slim.

It was going to be a little bit of a whirlwind for me on race weekend, as I couldn't afford to take much time off of work. And I had agreed to ride in the car with my parents, who are awesome and wanted to come up from Georgia and support me. My parents got to Nashville Thursday night, and we drove at 6:00 a.m. on Friday morning to head north. After about twelve hours and a few rush hours in various cities, we finally made it to Milwaukee just fifteen minutes before the prerace panel discussion at the local North Face store, which was led by some very well-known folks in the ultrarunning world—Timothy Olsen, Dylan Bowman, and Dean Karnazes! All of these guys are true warriors and ambassadors of our sport, so it was cool to see them up close and personal and to hear some cool stories and tips from them.

After that, it was time to head to the hotel, check in, pack my food/gear for the next morning, and catch a few hours of sleep. The alarm went off at 3:00 a.m., a time one should never see awake unless you have a 5:00 a.m. race start! My parents are troopers and got up with me. We ate breakfast and were soon on our way to the race start, about twenty minutes away. We made it in time to soak in the prerace atmosphere of fancy tents, bonfires, music and a slightly annoying announcer who shouted everything over his megaphone as if it were a NASCAR race. Before I knew it, we were off and running in the dark with our headlamps on, to the relative solitude of the trails.

I started out feeling pretty fresh and dialed into a steady pace that felt strong yet comfortable. Those early miles clipped by quickly with relative ease—just covering the gently rolling dirt and rock trails through the wooded parts of Kettle Moraine State Park. Things seemed to be going smoothly until about 10 miles in, when my stomach started to rebel. Knowing I would need to sacrifice a few minutes, I ducked off into the woods. And as I did so, my hat and headlamp got knocked off by a low-hanging branch. What I didn't realize until after I got back on the trail was that I had also dropped my GoPro camera! Once I realized that, I spent several minutes looking around for it, to no avail, and didn't want to sacrifice any more clock time to that search. So, unfortunately, I had to move on, sans camera.

Within a minute of ditching the GoPro, I came to a fork in the trail that was marked, but the marking was not clear on which way it was actually pointing! I waited a few seconds on the next runner, and we decided it looked like we should take the right split. After several minutes in that direction, with no trail markers, a group of runners came back to us, saying that they weren't sure that we were going the correct way. So we all backtracked to the original split and determined we should have gone the other way. All in all, I probably only lost ten to fifteen minutes with the bathroom / GoPro / off course triple whammy. But mentally, it felt like I had lost a lot of time that I had banked by strong pacing, and it felt like the wheels were coming off.

I did my best to brush off those brief setbacks and get back into a rhythm. After all, this was a 50-miler race, and daylight was just breaking way. The next miles were a blur, as I focused on maintaining a decent pace and getting to mile 21, which would be the first time I would see my parents again since the start of the race. The terrain had gradually changed from dirt and rock to wide grassy trails, and I was surprised that my legs were losing their freshness and starting to ache. I knew that meant I was in for a "fun" last 30 miles. Things were not going as ideally as I had hoped, but I finally reached the aid station at mile 21, still within the time frame I had estimated for my parents, and seeing their smiling faces always lifts the spirits!

After a few minutes to chow down at the aid station, it was time to head on a long out-and-back section of the course. I would return to the mile 21 aid station (and see the parents again) at mile 35. Within a mile of leaving mile 21, for me, I saw Tyler Sigle, who is the course record holder coming toward me hauling it, on his way back to mile 35. Man, that guy is superhuman! After a few more miles of wide grassy trails through the woods, we entered a long stretch of scenic open meadows, with large spans of waist-high grass, pretty yellow and purple flowers, and interspersed trees. This is what I internally called "the Beth Section." (See what I did there?) Several of my friends from Nashville were down in Chattanooga, Tennessee running their own race at that very moment, StumpJump 50K. I was thinking about all of them, cheering them on internally, while I was going through this cool section of trail.

My legs were feeling increasingly fatigued, and I was having continued stomach problems, but I did my best to chip away at the course and only walk when I started feeling really miserable. Honestly, I felt like I was doing terribly, until I neared the 50K mark on my Garmin watch (mile 31), and passed it in five hours, twenty-eight minutes. That was the second fastest time I'd ever covered that distance on foot! Not too shabby.

Somewhere, around the same time, I saw Dean Karnazes (another famous ultrarunner sponsored by the North Face, who had ran a marathon in every state in the United States, approximately one a week for a year; he's amazing!). Dean looked me in the eye and said, "Right on." If that doesn't give you a good kick in the rear, I don't know what will. After the adrenaline from seeing Dean wore off, I knew it was going to be a slow grind in the pain cave to the finish, as my legs truly felt terrible. I wanted nothing more than for the finish to be right in front of me. I saw my parents again at mile 35, stopped at the bathroom again, and also tried to get down some broth. I stuck primarily to my diet of Coke and potato chips though.

Those final fifteen miles were mostly repeated sections

of what we had covered before, with some fresh sections reminding me of the horse trails at Percy Warner park in Nashville. I just did my best to keep at a slow steady jog, breaking that up every couple of minutes with some hiking. I continued to feel increasing fatigue but still did my best to encourage others in passing and keep covering ground as efficiently as my body would allow.

Finally, some race volunteers or spectators said, "About a mile to go!" which was such a relief after a tough day! Somehow the worst-feeling legs can get rejuvenated when you know you only have a short distance to the finish. I was able to pick up the pace for the final half mile or so to cruise across the finish in a personal best time by over an hour at nine hours, twenty-eight minutes. Mission accomplished!

Free food at the finish; met a few more cool folks after the race; reconnected with a buddy made during the race; and to top it all off, my mom helped me find my GoPro camera when we went back to mile 10 on the course after the race!

***

Author's note: When we were done eating and talking after the race, it was still daylight. Since we had exhausted all efforts to find the GoPro camera at the lost and found, Steven said he thought he could find the part of the trail he had been on when he lost it. So Jay drove our Jeep back to the trail, with Steven riding up front to navigate us to a road near a white fence next to the trail. I sat in the back seat praying we'd have enough light to be able to search for it.

We pulled off the main highway, and Steven said, "Dad,

you can stay with the car, and Mom and I will go on the trail and look for the GoPro."

So off we went a few hundred yards into the woods. And since it was October, the trail was covered with thousands of leaves! Also there were several places where the trail branched off.

We separated and went over and around bushes and downed tree limbs. All the while, the sunlight was fading; our time having natural light was limited.

Then I had the thought, God knows where his GoPro is, and if He wants us to find it, He will show us where it is.

So Steven and I met back up and went a few feet farther on the trail, both looking down and scooting leaves around. That was when I saw a square metal face that had the words, "Hero II" on it. I looked up and asked Steven, "Does your gopro have the word Hero *on it?"*

He smiled. We both looked down and saw the camera, Steven picked it up, and I hugged him! Lots of prayers were answered in that moment! Thank you, Lord, for showing us the way! God will make a way when there seems to be no way.

***

All in all, NFCW50 was a scenic course that wasn't tough in elevation but challenged me to push through many mental and physical difficulties and appreciate the positives.

CHAPTER 10

The Road to UTMB, Chamonix, France, Part II

In fall 2015, Steven bought another property in Nashville, a house on Sabre Drive. He had renovated his condo from 2012 to 2014 and had an interest in acquiring something else—a new project to sink his teeth into. He had been looking at houses for sale in the Nashville area for several months, but moderately priced homes in his area were selling as soon as they were listed due to the influx of people moving to Nashville who needed housing. One day, he saw a listing on Sabre that didn't have a picture of the house yet. He knew where the house was and went to see it and then made an offer through his realtor. Later one of his friends said he didn't know how Steven had gotten that house in such a tight market. Steven told us that he thought the only reason there weren't multiple offers that day was because no photo of the house was on the listing. God's grace played a role again!

He moved to this house in November 2015 and renovated the kitchen and basement in the next several months. He rented out his condo to a friend. And through it all, he still worked at NRC and continued his training for runs leading up to his goal of eventually running in the UTMB.

Steven's 2016 races included a Chattanooga race in March with his RunWILD group; a trip to Bend, Oregon, and run with friends in June; the annual Tomato Run in Nashville in August; and the StumpJump with RunWILD in October.

He did apply for the lottery for running in UTMB in 2016 but was not chosen. Not to be deterred, Steven continued on with his home improvements and his running training. He also put together "a dream wall" in his living room, which included a picture of Mont Blanc in France (where UTMB is located). Never give up!

CHAPTER 11

The Road to UTMB, Chamonix, France, Part III

Whole30 Diet and Ultrarunning by Steven McNeal
February 3, 2017

As a New Year's resolution of sorts for 2017, I decided to give the Whole30 diet a go from January 1 through 30. This diet, which I will explain more about in a minute if you don't already know already about its rigid charm, presented quite a few challenges—including how to rework and structure my running nutrition. I wanted to write this post to share my experience and also to provide a resource to any long distance runners out there attempting the diet while training. If you just want to read about the nutrition aspect, feel free to skip down. If you are interested in reading about the diet and my experience with it, grab a (compliant) snack and read on!

So, to back up for a second, my running buddy Jeff Davis had been talking about high-fat / ketosis diet mumbo jumbo starting fall 2016. He was praising the benefits profusely during our morning runs, speaking of consistent energy levels, needing to eat less in general, and even reports of less stomach issues during ultraevents from other friends on this type of diet. Admittedly, Jeff had piqued my interest. Then when I saw one of my cousins (who is not a runner) over Thanksgiving, he was raving about the Whole30 diet, which is similar to the high-fat diet. I was sold. I'm leaving out a few details, but these two key people's testimonials, plus the fact that I felt exhausted all the time, somehow lit a fire underneath me to try this thing out.

If you followed the timeline there, you'll notice a gap from where I decided over Thanksgiving to when I actually started the diet in January. With me not knowing how to even start the diet or what to eat and with holiday food galore in the month of December, I decided to use December as a prep month with a start date of January 1. This actually worked out really well. Immediately after Thanksgiving, I ordered *It Starts with Food*, a book recommended by my cousin to explain the "whys" behind Whole30 food choices. Having the month of December allowed me to read through the book, to begin clearing out my pantry of any foods that weren't Whole30 compliant, and to start shopping for groceries that were approved. This soft entry was also helpful because the first trips to the grocery store when you're trying to make this diet for real can be a little overwhelming, because you're trying to sort through every ingredient of every food product—all the while using your phone to see if certain ingredients fit the bill or not.

So, here's a quick rundown of what the Whole30 diet is. Skip over this paragraph if you're already enlightened! From my read of *It Starts with Food*, it's basically seeking to give you a healthier relationship with food, leading to a healthier gut; reducing/eliminating any inflammation in your body; giving you more energy, alertness, longevity, and superpowers; and so on. To abide by the diet you have to eliminate *all* added sugar (including natural sugar such as honey), all alcohol, almost all dairy, al beans/legumes, all grains, and preservatives. So what *can* you eat? Grass-fed / wild-caught meats, certain oils, vegetables, fruits, tree nuts (not peanuts), and a few other odds and ends. And you can have coffee! Hallelujah! People like to ask me then, "So it's a no-carb diet right?" False. Vegetables and fruits have carbs! They are just good carbs loaded with nutrients and fiber. Quick side note: Whole30 also has a few other "rules," including not trying to combine approved ingredients to make desserts or comfort foods. They're trying to break emotional habits with those rules, and since my only goal was to feel more consistent energy and have my body be healthier, I did not abide by this rule. As long as all the ingredients I was consuming were compliant, I was perfectly content to say I was following the diet.

When I started the diet in January, I was already getting accustomed to buying items on the Whole30 list and cooking much, much more than I'd ever cooked before. I'll spare you the details of all the foods I made, but I do want to share a few surprising observations, even revelations, that I had during this thirty-day period.

First of all, I did not enjoy cooking before January. It felt like a chore, too much planning and too much *work*! Somehow, almost magically, I was forced to start cooking almost all of my meals to become compliant with this diet, and I actually started to *enjoy* cooking! I even (gasp) *almost* started enjoying going grocery shopping! That was my least favorite chore before Whole30. But suddenly grocery shopping and cooking were becoming adventures, where I sought out ways to create tasty meals that were good for my being and did actually change the way I related to food. I began to get excited about having an assortment of nutrient-rich foods arrayed on my counter and in my fridge. Food and eating was no longer a chore and block in the way of everything else I needed to do. Instead it was something I appreciated, looked forward to, and savored.

So did Whole30 give me increased energy and super running powers? Yes and no, not really. My primary goal of feeling better in general *did* happen, thankfully! I felt more consistent energy throughout each day and could sense an improvement in focus, sleep, and even emotional health. I observed that, even though I was spending more time cooking, overall I was more productive because I had more energy throughout the day. As for my running, I actually ran 70 miles my first week on Whole30, an activity not seemingly recommended. But that was my plan, and I was going to do it regardless.

Some people really struggle the first week or two on Whole30 because your body is purging and may feel sluggish, but I think my soft entry in December helped me to feel fine when I went on the diet in full force. I will say that, even though my running didn't feel greatly improved on any given day during the diet, I did feel like my recovery in general went better, which, in turn, allowed my running fitness to progress rather nicely during the month of January.

I could go on and on, but before I get too long-winded, I'll wrap up with what I discovered about how to create a workable nutrition plan for long runs on Whole30. Here's what my typical *pre*-Whole30 long run nutrition setup would normally look like: See picture.

And after several weeks of searching and scouring for decent portable foods that had all Whole30-approved ingredients, here's what my new Whole30 long run nutrition looks like: See picture.

You'll note that I had to cut out *everything* that I had eaten on runs before and totally rework the system. I found that I absolutely love nut butters (bring on the jokes), and really my favorite piece of nutrition in the new mix is Thunderbird bars. Seriously, I will continue to eat these as a very enjoyable snack. The RX bars are also quite tasty, even though the egg whites don't sound appealing for runs. Epic bars are another useful source of energy on runs; with low calories overall, I found that they digest quite easily. A surprise find was eating baby food. This could be mentally challenging for some, but I had no problem paying $1.20

for a pack of organic fruit/vegetables that tasted great. As an additional note to anyone training long distance, I found that when I tried to eat every thirty minutes, it was too much and built up in my stomach. I settled in on eating about one of these items per hour on my longer runs.

I'm sure there are many more options out there that could work on this diet, but hopefully this post will give some direction to anyone on this diet or just considering making changes to their running fuel lineup. I know that, for me, it even sparked an idea for my own nutrition business, which I'm really excited about!! More details to come on that in the future.

And one last note: I did allow myself one cheat day (technically I should have started the thirty days all over at that point) for my mom's birthday. Again, my goal with the diet was to feel better, not to punish myself. I ate an amazing grass-fed burger with bun and all, sweet potato fries, and birthday cake. I enjoyed it a lot and felt great!

CHAPTER 12

Move to Bend

J ay and I had a call from Steven in March and he said that he was going to do a long run in Sewanee, Tennessee, on a trail he'd ran many times before. He wondered if we wanted to meet him for lunch after his run in Sewanee at Dave's Modern Tavern there. We liked Dave's since it had a laidback atmosphere and good food, so we said that we would meet him there. Steven had lived in Sewanee in June and July 2004, after he graduated from Jacksonville State University and before he moved to Nashville. He was a part of the Summer Music Festival and played trombone in the orchestra there. It was a great summer experience and turned his thinking toward moving to Nashville and working there.

He had a double major in college, music and accounting, so he devised a plan to use both and work in accounting at the Nashville Symphony. After the Sewanee music festival, he made a work proposal and got an interview with Michael, the head of accounting at the symphony, and pitched his idea. It was accepted, and he had the job! In August 2004, he moved to Nashville and had lived there for thirteen years by this time.

When we met him at Dave's Tavern, we thought it was just for a nice lunch. But after we'd eaten, Steven said he had something to tell us. Jay and I looked at each other and thought, *What now?*

Steven told us he was planning on moving to Bend, Oregon, in June, initially to train in high altitude for UTMB for a few months but maybe longer. It was a real surprise, actually a shock; we hadn't expected this news. But God would help us through this. It would just take time to get used to the idea. The post that follows is Steven's take on his move.

Mirror Ponding on My Move to Bend by Steven McNeal August 22, 2017

As you probably know, a few months ago, I picked up my life from Nashville and made the big move to Bend, Oregon. Actually, I didn't so much pick up my life as leave everything to start over in a sense. Nashville treated me fairly well over the past decade or so, albeit with some serious ups and downs that tend to happen in life. I worked my initial dream job with the Nashville Symphony, played music seriously for several years and taught at a private school, got addicted to running and ultramarathons, endured several rounds of love and heartache, purchased and renovated three properties, and made lots of amazing friends in Nashville. I plugged in to various types of communities in Nashville over the years, starting with musicians and churchgoers. And over time, my main jam was predominantly the running community.

I am thankful for my time with all of those communities and the friends there, many of which will be lifelong. But I somehow reached a point where I felt stuck in a rut, doing the same things (mostly good things), and I couldn't seem to escape haunting memories and reminders of disappointments I've had while in Nashville. And then there's the humidity in the summer! I swear I get seasonal depression every summer! Even though I had built up quite a life in Nashville, I really needed a change and a fresh start. This quote from Henry Cloud captures the essence of why I moved: "We change our behavior when the pain of staying the same becomes greater than the pain of changing."

Enter Bend. I had visited the town in 2016 with my buddy Daniel and fell in love with the place almost instantly. With generally more temperate summers (at least it's a dry heat and cools down at night) and mountains and trails galore, it's a pretty cool town. I also like the size; it's less than a hundred thousand in population, making traffic a bit easier but still having plenty of entertainment options. So I gradually made plans for the move, including getting rid of thousands of dollars worth of old inventory from a failed business I had, finishing renovating my house in Nashville to get ready to rent out, and purging most of my belongings with the goal of fitting whatever was leftover in my new vehicle that I also bought for my move out West.

I was blown away by the support and love shown me by friends as I prepared for the big change. But it needed to be done, and I finally set off on my cross-country drive in mid-May.

My journey across the country for the move truly was epic and unforgettable. I had planned most of the trip before

I left, but added in even more things along the way. I ran races all three weekends on my trip—a half marathon after my first night in Kansas, a 50-miler at the Grand Canyon, and a last-minute decision for a 22-mile mountain race in Idaho. I spent a few days in Denver and Boulder with family and friends; a few days exploring around Zion, Bryce, and Antelope Canyon with my good buddy Mayne; and too many other fun mini-explorations and stops with friends to list here. I had an absolute blast on the drive out, but by the end, after almost three full weeks of travel, I was ready to get to Bend.

When I finally arrived in my new world of Bend, my new roommate, Julie (former East Nasty for Life running group friend), had cleared space in her apartment for me and was very welcoming, going out for food on my first evening in town. I immediately started hopping into running groups and looking for job opportunities. I had moved here without a set job but plenty of ideas and backgrounds to work with. I really enjoyed those first weeks exploring my new surroundings and gradually making some new friends. I could even run from the apartment in Bend and hit the river trail and downtown, where the river pools into what we call Mirror Pond, in case you were wondering about my blog title (punny, I know). I fortunately also have had several Nashville friends visiting Bend over my first several months here, which has been awesome! I even went on spontaneous trips with some of these people from Bend to northern California, Portland, Oregon, and Seattle as part of their extended travels.

As amazing as life in Bend is and has the potential to be, I have to burst anyone's bubble who is under the illusion that I am living a glamorous life of running up mountains every day, floating on the Deschutes River with a drink in my hand in the high-desert sun in the afternoon, and going out every night laughing with newfound friends. The reality is, it's a struggle. Life will always have some element of this push and pull, and I never expect to land a perfect life, but this new phase and location has presented new challenges for me.

Work life in Bend was precarious at first. I scoured over job postings and craigslist ads for weeks, with little inspiration to chomp on many of the opportunities, but I did send my résumé / cover letter out to a few places. I had one interview, which I ended up turning down on the spot because it didn't feel like the right fit. Fortunately, I have been able to successfully start back up an Amazon-based business buying and reselling products. The process for that took over a month to get going and is super slow building any momentum, but it seems to be starting to work, finally! I have a lot of money invested in new inventory and very little cash flow to show for it, but sales are on the upswing, thankfully. That being said, I have bills to pay here and am steadily incurring more debt. So, for now, I am limiting spending and not going out more than a couple of times a week. Most of my days are filled with early-morning coffee at my apartment, followed by either sourcing inventory (shopping) or preparing inventory at my place to send in to Amazon, followed by cooking dinner at home. I'm pretty confident that September will officially be the first month here where I make more than I spend.

And then there's running. A big part of why I made the transition to Bend was for the incredible and diverse landscapes and trails out here. I think before I moved I actually did picture myself eating mountains for breakfast out here daily. But the harsh reality is, shortly after moving to Bend, I just started being exhausted and fatigued all the time—like every run feels like I have a gorilla on my back, bricks on my feet, and a vise grip on my heart and lungs. My body isn't responding well, and I can't pinpoint for sure what's going on yet. But it's making running unfun, which is a shame with all this beauty around me. I can't even run a nine-minute mile on flat ground aerobically. In spite of how I've been feeling, I have had some amazing (views and experience-wise) runs/hikes with friends out here. And I think I may be on track to feeling better with incorporating more rest and a big diet change that I am trying with high-fat, primal style foods. I mostly eat at home, but I'm confident that I'll be getting out more in due time.

Did I mention that I'm in training for the Mountain Lakes 100-miler next month? It's on September 23 and 24. With how my running has been going, it's pretty concerning for me, even though this will be my third 100-mile race. But I would rather do my best to get there well rested and undertrained, rather than with dead legs that have put in too many miles for their own good. This will be by far the least mileage I've done for a 100-miler, but you can be darn sure I will do everything in my power to get myself ready in this next month, even if it means more rest. I will be on that start line, and I'm excited to see some new trails, make some new ultra friends, have my parents come out to crew, and give it my best effort. The goal is to earn this beauty, the Mountain Lakes 100 belt buckle.

If you've managed to read this far, thanks for being

interested in my life. Like I said, it's a struggle at the moment. But at least it's a struggle, and struggle is a verb. It's active. I don't give up easily, and I'm constantly trying to fight my way to a better life. I need community to support me along the way in that, and I'm super thankful for continued support from old friends, my family, and new friends I'm making here in Bend. So I raise my imaginary glass to you all for being there for me and look forward to catching up soon. I'll be back in Nashville and Georgia sometime around the holidays. Cheers!

CHAPTER 13

The Road to UTMB, Chamonix, France, Part IV

2017 Mountain Lakes 100 by Steven McNeal
October 6, 2017

This is ultimately a race report, but just describing race weekend alone would be a very incomplete picture of my overall experience. So first, a bit of backstory. My love affair with the beauty of Oregon began in June 2016 when I ran The NUT 100K trail race by Go Beyond Racing (they also put on Mountain Lakes 100). The NUT almost took me out of commision when I had the bonk of all bonks, but I survived and made a new friend, Brian. who helped me through the final 18 plus miles. After that race, Brian ran Mountain Lakes 100 in September 2016 and had good things to say about it, so ML100 was solidly on my radar. It's also been a dream of mine to run the UTMB 100 in the Alps of Europe some day, and completing ML100 gives you some much-needed points for UTMB. So when registration opened up for Mountain Lakes, I was on it! And good thing, because it sold out quickly for 2017!

My plan for training for ML100 had been to put in some serious miles throughout the summer and explore the many varied trails and scenery Oregon has to offer, which should have been easy to accomplish since I moved to Bend in Central Oregon in June. *But*, as you may have read about in my previous blog post on my move to Bend [Chapter 12], just as soon as I got to Bend, I started experiencing a lethargy and fatigue that I just couldn't seem to shake for several months. My average training paces went from 8:30/mile to 10:00/mile. I couldn't seem to manage more than 40 miles/week without feeling like my legs had been through a meat grinder.

So I started focusing on what I could control—my diet and more rest. I started incorporating more rest days (non-running) into my schedule, trying my best to listen to my body's needs rather than the mileage on my schedule. Also, I simply didn't set an alarm most mornings, unless I was meeting friends for an early run. And I made sure to get to bed at a reasonable hour too. And as for diet, my eating habits and beliefs have undergone a massive transformation over the past year. I really started to focus on a primal diet in the six weeks leading up to the Mountain Lakes 100. My running buddy Jeff Davis cued me in to this type of eating, sharing his success and the success of other friends on this type of diet preparing for ultras. Basically, you cut out grains, added/refined sugars, and vegetable oils. Then you focus on eating organic grass-fed meats, nuts, coconut products, healthy fats, and vegetables. When you eat this way, it teaches your body to burn a higher percentage of fats and a lower percentage of carbs at any given effort. Since you get more efficient at using fat for fuel, you don't need to take in as many calories during longer efforts, and your body can focus less on digestion and more on the task at hand. I could go on and on about this, but one of the key resources that helped me was *Primal Endurance*, a book by Mark Sisson that covers pretty much everything about eating primally as it relates to endurance training.

The changes to my diet definitely helped my general life energy levels throughout each day. But going into Mountain Lakes, I still didn't have the big mileage weeks or any speed whatsoever in my legs. I did get in two 60-mile weeks and a couple of 25-mile days as my longest training runs. I finally started to feel rested during my taper and also threw in some leg strength workouts two weeks before the race, with the final workout about a week before to make sure I was fully rested.

Race weekend finally had arrived. And on Friday, I drove the three hours from Bend to Olallie Lake, arriving just in time for the prerace dinner. After eating, picking up my race bib and swag, and mingling with other runners, I returned to my abode for the night, my Nissan Pathfinder. I'd never slept in my car before, so I wasn't sure how it would work out the night before, waking to run 100 miles. I chatted briefly with my friendly car neighbors, Mary and Jory, who were also sleeping in their car and running in the race. At least we were all in the same boat, so to speak! Fortunately, the car camping area was dark and relatively quiet by around 8:00 p.m., and I slept pretty well most of the night and stayed pretty warm, even though the temps dipped pretty close to the low forties / high thirties.

I woke up just before my 6:00 a.m. alarm, feeling rested and ready to go. After throwing on some warm clothes and cooking up a quick breakfast over my camp stove, I moseyed down to the start area about 50 yards away. I spotted my friend Chris, who I had run with in Portland a few times, and chatted with him as we awaited the prerace instructions. Daylight had started around 6:30, so by the time Todd and Renee started briefing us around 7:45, the day was cool and bright. One thing I *love* about ultras, and 100-milers in particular, is the indescribable energy that is in the air at the race start. You can tangibly feel the excitement amid the teeth chattering in the crisp morning, as Todd counted down to the start. Every one of us has our own story, but we have all prepared so much in our own ways. And to bottle up all that preparation and unleash it at the start of a 100 is an amazing feeling. After the countdown and some cheers of pure exhilaration, we were off and moving.

Todd had warned us about snow covering most of the first 26 miles of the course, since it had snowed six inches a few days before. In addition, there was a rerouted section due to the forest fires in the area. I had covered the first 26 miles of the course on my own a month prior to the race in my own training to scope out the course, and I can't tell you how much that helped me out. I knew that the first 26 was probably the most difficult on the course, and I also knew that the course change cut out the faster fire road section in exchange for a more rugged, albeit beautiful trail. So I knew going in that this first quarter of the race with snow cover would be very slow for me. I had vowed to keep my effort to no more than a 6 out of 10 the entire race, as I blew up in my last hundred when I went out too fast.

Sticking to my plan, I incorporated hiking within the first miles of jeep road as we hit uphill sections leading us to the trail. I overheard some Canadians talking about visiting Bend soon, so of course I chimed in and ended up offering suggestions for their upcoming visit. Before we knew it, we were on the trail, moving steadily through snow. Thankfully, the majority of the runners in front of us had trampled down a lot of the snow, so it really didn't slow me down too much. I love the pureness that snow adds to any landscape, and it was a treat to be able to run in it with only shorts and a T-shirt after warming up in the first few miles. After a while, a runner passed me that I thought I recognized from one of my training runs near Bend. Sure enough, it was him that I had seen on one of my last long runs! Christopher and I ended up sharing some good miles together, which was a pleasant distraction from the melting snow puddles that were forming on the trail.

I rolled back up to Olallie Lake (mile 26) still feeling pretty fresh in just under eight hours, which was right in line with my pacing plan. If you do the math, a sub-thirty hour finish at this rate does not sound promising. But I knew that the beginning section would be the slowest, and I still felt fantastic since I had kept my effort easy, so I didn't panic. My parents were there to help me, so it was great to see them and sit for a few minutes in a camp chair while they brought me anything I wanted.

***

Author's note: When we first saw Steven at mile 26, he looked so good—full of energy and strength! A few of the other runners were telling their crew members that they couldn't believe how hard the first 26 miles were, and they were probably going to drop out. His training plan and eating regimen were proving to be working so far. Lots of prayers were helping too.

***

Shortly, after eight hours of elapsed time, I high-fived the race director and got back moving.

I knew that the coming miles would be where my new nutrition strategy would be put to the test. In my previous 200-mile races, I had bonked at mile 30-something and mile 28. Both bonks were mostly stomach related, as I had been able to rally after a long period of bonk and finish both events.

I kept my mantra of "conserve" going, and never let myself panic about pace. Now we were on the long section of the Pacific Crest Trail (PCT), which we would again do in the opposite direction after circling Timothy Lake later on. Luckily, the snow was minimal on the PCT, and most of the terrain was rolling but not too technical. I was still feeling good, so I picked up the pace (but not the effort) on a lot of the flats and downhills.

Eventually, I caught up to another runner who I had bumped into several times earlier in the race, who always acknowledged my name each time.Turns out, his name was Stephen, so he had a fairly easy way to remember! Stephen had been running with his buddy earlier, who had ended up lagging behind due to an IT band issue. He informed me that it was his first night run (crazy!). So since our names and paces aligned, we ended up running together through most of the night section.

It was great to have company through the night hours and, as often happens for me when I'm running with friends, I often forget to eat as often as I should. I noticed that I was getting hungry as we were between aid stations but decided to wait to eat until we got to the next AS. As often happens, it was a little longer than expected, and I arrived superhungry. This particular aid station had quesadillas and bacon. Need I say more? I ended up overeating a little, and this was the only time I felt nausea during the entire race. I told Stephen I needed to walk a little coming out of the aid, and within ten minutes, the nausea wore off and I was ready to roll.

After some more steady miles with Stephen and another friend Jeremy for a while, we finally finished the PCT section and hit Clackamas Ranger Station at mile 55 before the Timothy Lake loop. Stephen had his girlfriend at Clackamas to assist and introduced us with a kind offer for her to help me also. Around this time, one of the volunteers, Shannon, approached me and just started helping me with whatever I needed. You can tell when a volunteer is an ultrarunner, because he or she asks really astute questions and can practically tell you what you need before you even ask. Shannon had run ML100 last year and also Western States, so she knew the drill and set me up for success. After fueling up and putting on some warmer gear (since it was cooling off more as it got deeper into the night), I started off shortly behind Stephen on the next section of trail, starting around Timothy Lake. I caught up with Stephen and stayed with him for a short while. It was getting into the wee hours of the morning, so both of us were getting a little tired, and the conversation was naturally a little more spread out. Stephen's hips and achilles were nagging him a little, so he was walking a bit more now. I was still feeling like running some more, so I let him know I was going to run ahead and would probably see him later.

The Timothy loop is about 16 miles total, including a short out-and-back section from Clackamas to the lake. I kept a steady pace running most of the flats and downhills and hiking the ups. There are two aid stations going around the lake, and I only paused for about five minutes at the first one to get some warm broth and snacks in me. After a few more miles of running solo, I arrived at the second aid around Timothy and was surprised by hearing a familiar voice, my friend Brian from the NUT 100K! I knew Brian was at the event pacing our mutual friend Chris, but I didn't realize I would see Brian at this point, so it was a welcome sight to have a friend waiting on me in the stark night.

After sitting and catching up with Brian for a few, he gave

me the boot, and I was back on my way toward Clackamas. This section between the dam and Clackamas had a little more uphill than I'd expected, but I was still feeling decent and moved well. Finally I finished the lake loop and had returned to the out-and-back section between the lake and Clackamas. At one point, you cross a road, which creates a clearing in the trees. All alone, I paused and turned off my headlamp, looking up to admire the spectacular starry night sky. I could see Orion shining brightly, and all was quiet and still. Sometimes little moments like those remind you why you're out there. "Be still and know I am your God."

When I made it back to Clackamas Ranger Station at mile 71, Shannon again made sure I got an appropriate amount of food in and went through a checklist of gear and upcoming course profile to ensure I was ready for the remaining overnight hours. I set off after a few minutes and started tackling the next mostly uphill section. I kept waiting on my stomach to rebel or for the inevitable bonk to happen, as it almost always has in any ultra I have ever done. I made it to the next aid station, Red Wolf, which was the quesadilla aid station. I wised up and asked for half of a quesadilla and one slice of bacon. That amount sat well in my stomach as I made my way out. During this next section, it was the coldest part of the night, but the first signs of daylight mercifully began. I embrace the night as part of the journey in a 100, but it sure is nice when the day starts anew and you start to hear signs of life all around you again!

I almost wish I had some drama to report here to make for a more interesting story, but honestly, the remainder of the race went really well. My stomach held up, great thanks to my efforts with my prerace diet, and the only real struggle I had was coping with the inevitable fatigue from sleep deprivation and sheer time on feet. The rolling hills and sporadic sweeping valley views of the PCT helped to distract me from any discomfort. And since things were going relatively well at this point in the race, I really did my best to appreciate and soak in all the beauty surrounding me.

Clicking off the final few aid stations like clockwork, I made it to the final aid station at mile 97 with plenty of time to spare (to finish before the cutoff time). I knew if I kept a steady rhythm for the final section, I had a pretty good shot at coming in to the finish in under twenty-nine hours. I also knew that my parents and a warm breakfast were waiting for me at the finish, as added motivation. Hey, anything that works, right? Fortunately, the smell of eggs and bacon (mostly imaginary) bolstered me onward, and I passed a few other runners in that final section, offering encouragement that we were all going to get there at that point. Finally, I reached the end of our PCT stint and was met by cheers from bystanders on the homestretch of dirt road. When I heard Mom shouting, "Go, Steven!" I couldn't help but smile and let out a sigh of relief as I crossed through the finish chute, coming through in twenty-eight hours and fifty-four minutes.Todd and Renee greeted me with warm smiles and a shiny new belt buckle. You can just tell that they are so glad that all of us are out there, and they, the volunteers, do everything in their power to get you across that finish line! So a huge thanks to them and also, again, thank you to my amazing parents for driving across the country to be there for me and with me.

(As a side note, I waited and watched the final hour of finishers, hoping to see my new buddies, Christopher and

CHAPTER 14

Our 2017 Trip out West to See Steven in the Mountain Lakes 100 in Oregon

On Sunday afternoon, September 17, 2017, we left our home in Summerville, Georgia, to begin our journey to Bend, Oregon, to see our son, Steven, during his third 100-mile race. We went north on I-59 and then west on I-24 toward Nashville (where Steven lived from 2004 until 2017). Steven still owns a condo and a house in Nashville, so we drove by his house on our way. He has three male renters there now (two of them are named Zach and Matthew, our grandsons' names). But no one was there at the house when we got there. So I got out of the car and took a picture of the house to send to Steven. When I texted the picture to Steven, he responded with a happy face emoji and said that was cool that we had gone by there. Even though he has a property management company taking care of his properties, it still helps him to see them for himself every few months, and everything looked good.

We spent our first night in Bowling Green, Kentucky, drove through Illinois, and then ate lunch at a Red Lobster in St. Louis, Missouri. It was so delicious!

After lunch, it rained really hard for a while and was very cloudy until we got to Kansas. Then the sun came out. In Topeka, Kansas, we got to our hotel and parked. Next door, we saw a Freddy's restaurant. So, after checking in, we walked over and ate there. There were several young families there, and we enjoyed our meal. (My father had clued us in to Freddy's in Florida because he liked their hamburgers. He was a World War II veteran, and so was Freddy. Their custard ice cream is good too.) We went back to our hotel and watched TV and slept. The next morning, we watched the morning news and saw a sunrise over Manhattan, Kansas, on the weather report. Steven has been to Manhattan several times on his various trips out west from Nashville. His friend Luke's parents live there, and Steven has been a guest of theirs each time. His last car trip there, he also ran in a half marathon in Manhattan.

After breakfast, we drove west through more of Kansas. Our goal for the day was to get to Denver, Colorado, before dinnertime so that we could visit with my sister, Leigh Anne, and her husband, Stanley. They had lived in Denver for about a year and a half.

In 2015, when we drove out West to Utah to see Steven run in the Bryce Canyon 100, we had stopped in Abilene, Kansas, to see the Eisenhower Memorial. We decided to stop in Abilene again because we had enjoyed it so much before, and we had plenty of time before we needed to be in Colorado. Since it was several minutes before the information center would be open, we walked over to the chapel. Once inside, we saw beautiful stained glass windows and a three-sided granite wall with inscriptions of Dwight Eisenhower's inspirational quotes.

Below the wall were the crypts where he and his wife, Mamie, and one of their children are buried.

We said a prayer for our family there and then went outside and around a beautiful fountain. Then we walked on a sidewalk to a two-story white house that was Eisenhower's childhood home. Later, we watched a black-and-white biographical film of his life in the information center.

After leaving, we went through Kansas and on to Denver, where we stayed with my sister and brother-in-law in their beautiful condo near downtown Denver with a panoramic view of the city. We walked to a nearby restaurant and had a lovely meal and great conversation.

The next morning, we ate, and Stanley helped us with directions out of the city and on to I-80. It was Steven's thirty-eighth birthday—September 20, 2017! So I posted a picture of Steven standing on top of a mountain and a message—"Happy Birthday, Steven."

Many people liked it and wished him good luck on his upcoming race. The prayers and good wishes of friends are priceless!

Beth, one of his friends and RunWILD running group leader. commented on his picture and said, "Happy birthday, Steven. And next time, please answer your Facetime calls." It turns out that she had gotten several of their runner friends together to wish him Happy birthday, and he hadn't been able to answer. Oh well. He plans to go to Nashville while he is home for Thanksgiving, so he will see many of his friends in person then.

We drove on through Wyoming, where it dropped to thirty-five degrees and then went on to Ogden, Utah, for the night. The tire pressure on our car tires was reading low. So the next morning, Jay and I went to the gas station beside our hotel and got our tires filled with air. Later we found out that it was just due to the temperature outside dropping and that we were okay.

The last day of long driving was to Ontario, Oregon, just across the Oregon state line. We drove through Idaho and stopped in Twin Falls at a Perkins restaurant for lunch. Then we made it to the Oregon state line by 4:50 mountain time. We stopped at the Oregon welcome center, and it was five minutes until 5:00 pm closing time. But the lady running the center was very welcoming and let us choose a couple of pamphlets on Bend, Oregon. Then we drove on to our hotel a few minutes away.

We checked into our hotel and then drove a few blocks to a Panda Express and had dinner. Then we walked to a Walmart close by to get crackers and chips for snacks while we would be at Steven's race in the next few days. As we were leaving Walmart, we saw our first Oregon sunset! It was beautiful!

That day I had texted our daughter, Amy (who lives in Japan with her family), about our trip, and she was excited that we were in Oregon.

I texted Steven a picture of the "Welcome to Oregon" sign, and he liked it. He said that he hadn't remembered that sign. So I told him it wasn't on the highway but was in front of the welcome center. We were really excited that we'd get to see him tomorrow!!

On Friday, September 22, 2017, Jay and I left Ontario,

Oregon, in the cold and rainy dark morning at 6:30 a.m. After getting gas at a Love's station, I drove about 130 miles to Burns, Oregon. On the way there, we saw purple mountains! They looked like they were covered in velvet. The song "America the Beautiful" came to mind as I took in the "purple mountain majesties above the fruited plain." It brought tears to my eyes; the mountains were so pretty! We passed the Gold Creek, which looked like a small river flowing through the mountains.

After eating hash browns at a McDonald's, we left Burns and later stopped at a rest area where a sign said, "This rest area is closed from Nov 1 to April 1 due to weather conditions." We also saw many signs about where to change snow chains on cars/trucks. Later, we found out that the state of Oregon is environmentally conscious and does not salt its roads in winter; they just use snowplows. So people need snow tires or chains to be able to get around in winter. Good to know.

When we got to the apartment, Steven was bringing his hydration vest for the race the next day out to his car. We saw his new Oregon license plate on the front. Oregon car tags have a Christmas tree in the middle of the numbers. It's really a pine tree and looks pretty. Steven hugged us and said he was really glad to see us. Then he helped us carry in our bags. We talked for a while and then said that we could eat lunch at "Brother John's" before he had to leave for the race.

He said it was the same restaurant that he and Daniel had eaten at when he'd first visited Bend a couple of years ago. The weather was nice, and the food was so good!

Steven drove our car and took us for a tour around Bend. We saw the Victorian Cafe, the flag bridge over the Deschutes River, and the Old Mill where several nice stores are located. Steven went inside REI to get a collapsible coffee cup to use at his race. Then he drove us to a local gas station to get gas for our car. He told us that, in Oregon, most gas stations have attendants to pump your gas.

After we got back to the apartment, Steven got more gear together for the race the next day. He showed us the back interior of his Pathfinder where he had made a bed out of pillows, a sleeping bag, and blankets. It looked comfortable!

He was going to take eggs to cook for breakfast on his camp stove. I had made a pumpkin bread for him and brought it in our cooler. Steven wanted to eat a slice before he left, so I cut a piece for him and me and Jay, and we ate together.

Steven had also highlighted the roads for us on an Oregon map and printed out directions to the race. After talking about this, it was time for him to leave for the Mountain Lakes race site so that he could be there before dark. There would be no cell reception after Detroit, Oregon, a couple of hours from Bend. We hugged him goodbye and said that we would see him tomorrow at mile 26 (also the start/finish). God protect Steven during his race and help him with his stomach and his endurance. Watch over him and protect him. Give him people to talk to and be around while he is running. Thank you, Jesus. Keep him safe.

Mountain Lakes 100 Race Day
September 23, 2017

Jay and I got up on Saturday morning, got ready, and ate breakfast. We left Bend at 9:48 a.m. so that we could be at the race start / mile 26 / finish before 2:00 p.m. in order to see Steven there. (Steven had calculated the approximate time he would be coming through mile 26 and told us when to be there. So there was math involved in the timing of points on the race courses.)

It was a three-hour trip through Sisters, Oregon, and Detroit, Oregon, (where we lost all cell service for two days) and then twenty-five more miles until the sign for Olallie Lake and the race start. The last eight miles were over a gravel road with dozens of deep potholes that had to be driven around or gone over at zero miles an hour.

And not only did we traverse that gravel road; Jay and I got lost when we took a right turn, according to our GPS, and ended up on a logging road for a few miles. We turned around and went further on the main road until we saw the tiny sign (one foot by one foot) for Olallie Lake. Whew! What a relief to see cars and people at the end of that gravel road! Civilization at last!

But where were we going to park? There was a line of cars alongside the race trail about twenty to thirty cars long. The next place to park was up a hill past the cabins and behind where the runners parked. We wouldn't be able to see him from that spot. So then we turned around and saw the perfect place at the very beginning of the first line of cars. Jay was able to back into that place, and I thought, *We're going to stay here because we'll never find a more accessible place.*

It was 2:15 p.m., and Steven had told us he would probably be at mile 26 between 3:30 and 4:00 p.m. So we got out our camping chairs and placed them about 100 feet from the mile 26 aid station, where the volunteers had fruit, snacks, and sandwiches for the runners. We saw lots of runners come through. A few of the runners coming through the aid station said it was very snowy and much harder going than they had expected, since it had snowed six inches the previous night. We learned later that several dropped out of the race at that station.

At about 3:45 p.m., we saw Steven run up hill toward us and the aid station. He looked good. I got his drop bag (with his headlamp for the upcoming night hours), and he got out his charger to charge his GPS watch for the time he would be eating at the aid station. He ate some goldfish crackers and orange slices and drank water. After about ten to fifteen minutes, Steven said he was feeling good and started back on the trail. He greeted two of his friends, Christopher from Bend and Stephen from Denver. Then we told Steven that we were going to spend the night in our car. He gave Jay his car key and said we could use blankets from his car if we needed them. We found out later that Steven had gotten help from Shannon, a volunteer at Clackamas aid station during the night hours. Thank you, Jesus!

Steven had, thoughtfully, bought a new gray Columbia down coat with a fur-lined hood for me at the outlet in Bend. He told me that he knew I didn't have a coat warm enough for "winter" weather in Oregon. That coat was so comfortable and warm! I wore it all night with the hood up and all the next day. Jay and I slept in the front seats of our car for the night. Jay would start the engine and let it run to warm up the car for a few minutes every hour. We had plenty of blankets and would look up at all the thousands of stars in the night sky. So beautiful!

Around 3:15 a.m., we saw a runner with a headlamp go by the front of our car. Later we learned that he was the first-place finisher, Zach, thirty-eight years old, from Oregon.

In the next few hours, we saw some more runners come through to the finish in the dark. Then at 7:00 a.m., we went to the start/finish area to check things out.

Several tables were set up, and volunteers were cooking eggs, bacon, and hash brown Idaho potatoes. It looked great after a night of eating peanut butter crackers and snack cookies. There was also a table set up with coffee and hot water for tea or hot chocolate. Jay got a cup of coffee, and I got a cup of hot water and added a pack of hot chocolate mix to it. It tasted so warm and delicious.

In about an hour, some of the volunteers said that the food was ready. Several of the runners and crew and family got plates. Jay and I took our plates back to our car to eat so that we could run the engine and get our feet warm.

(It turned out that we had about five more hours to wait until Steven would come through the finish.)

For the next few hours, we mostly stayed in our car to stay warm, only getting out once an hour to walk around and exercise our legs. Around twelve noon, we got our camp chairs out of our trunk and sat outside and talked to other people waiting for their runners to come to the finish. About 12:54 p.m., I saw Steven through the pine trees, on the trail running toward the finish. I recognized his hat first, dark brown with a red Avalanche logo on it. I ran around spectators, rocks, a few dogs, and other obstacles, calling his name and taking a few pictures as I went to meet him at the finish line. The finish at the Mountain Lakes race is so beautiful, with an archway right at the lake shore and a perfect view of Mt. Bachelor in the distance.

It's easy to see the attraction—why people want to run in this race.

At the finish, the race director gave Steven his 100-mile Mountain Lakes belt buckle. Then his friend, Shannon, the volunteer who had helped him so much during the race, ran up to Steven and gave him a big hug. It was a special moment and shows the true spirit of this race, where volunteers do everything in their power to help their friends complete it and enjoy the experience.

Thank you, Jesus, for helping Steven complete this race and for protecting him and all the other people there.

Some of the "loot" he got for finishing this race included a nice blue T-shirt (blue-gray color with the Mountain Lakes logo on it), two stickers for his car with the logo, a glass with the logo, wool socks that he wore during the race, and a pair of bright orange Nike trail running shoes! One of the race directors said that, "Yes. Nike is a really good sponsor of the race." It was very fitting, since the Nike brand began in Oregon, around the time of Steve Prefontaine in the 1970s.

Some of the statistics about this race were reported as follows: Out of 152 runners that began the race, there were 81 finishers, and 71 DNF (did not finish), a 45 percent success rate.

Steven placed number 63 out of the 81 finishers. We are very proud of him and so glad that he finished feeling well, only tired. This was his first ultrarace where he did not get physically ill. He attributes the success to his nutrition and paleo diet of several months prior to the race. Also, he trained on the actual race course, the first 26 miles, a few weeks before the actual race when he drove to Olallie Lake by himself and ran those miles alone. Wow! This especially impressed me when I saw how desolate those miles were, after the runners left the lake area.

Steven has been disciplined and able to achieve success in many areas his whole life. God protect him and bless him in all his decisions.

After Steven changed his clothes and ate a good breakfast and talked to several people, we packed up his car and our car and headed back to Bend, a three and a half hour-drive. We ate dinner at Panda Express in Bend and then drove to his condo. By that time, he had been awake for over thirty-eight hours, running 100 miles during that time. We all slept great that night!

The day after the race was always my favorite day! In 2015, after his Bryce Canyon 100 mile, we drove to the North Rim of the Grand Canyon. It was great! On this Monday, after his Mountain Lakes 100, we went to Steven's favorite restaurant in Bend, the Victorian Cafe. We were seated at a nice booth by a window, and we could see the outside seating area where there were comfortable couches with burnt orange pillows and a working firepit. We ordered breakfast. Steven ordered the "18-wheeler with biscuits, gravy, scrambled eggs, fried potatoes and coffee."

He said that runners could burn up to fifteen thousand calories during a 100-mile race. Well, it was about a fifteen thousand-calorie breakfast, so he was on his way to regain some of the calories that he had used at the race. Jay had the bacon, egg, and blueberry pancake breakfast, and I had French toast. It was delicious!

Then Steven took us to the Old Mill District and the Flag Bridge. We took some pictures of us standing on the bridge over the Deschutes River. We went back to the condo and had delicious oat bread sandwiches with Oregon berry spread and almond butter, prepared by Steven. We watched a movie on Netflix while Steven checked his business results online. In the evening, we went to REI and then ate at a mexican restaurant in the Old Mill area. Jay got a Mexican Coca-Cola in a half-liter bottle. I had a taste, and it was very good. Steven and Jay had the chicken soup with avocados, chicken, and tomatoes. When I tasted it, I found it very warm and comforting. I had homemade guacamole with chips. After dinner, we walked around the Old Mill area and onto the Flag Bridge again. We decided to go to a movie, *Despicable Me 3* and waited until it was time for it to begin. In the meantime, Steven said he was hungry again (still trying to regain calories), so when we saw a Ben and Jerry's ice cream shop, we went inside and got ice cream cups. Then we went outside to eat it on picnic benches. After eating it, we went to the movie and enjoyed it. Then we drove back to the condo and went to sleep. Thank you, Lord, for a day of recovery and rest and fun!

On Tuesday, September 26, 2017 (the next day), we had a good day in Bend, another day of rest before we traveled to California. In the morning, Steven said he wanted us to go to Sparrow restaurant for breakfast. When we got there, it reminded me of a restaurant in East Nashville called Mongo Java. We ordered breakfast croissants for Jay and Steven and ham and cheese quiche for me.

After breakfast, we got our oil changed, since we had driven three thousand miles in two weeks. Then we drove up a winding road to Pilot Butte, about 500 feet above downtown Bend. Steven told us that Bend, Oregon, is about 3,500 feet above sea level, so Pilot Butte is 4,000 feet above sea level. At the top of Pilot Butte, there was an observation area with a brass dial plaque that was like a clock with straight lines pointing to different mountains in the area.

We learned that a caldera is a depression in the ground made thousands of years ago by volcanic activity. Steven told us that a butte is taller than it is wide, and a mesa is wider than it is tall. Jay says that mesa means table in Spanish. There was a sign that said the last time there was a volcanic eruption in that part of Oregon was 1,300 years ago. But there is potential of an eruption every 300 to 3,000 years. So it could happen any time—hopefully not when we're there, ha ha.

Steven told us that all of the mountains around there were volcanic, including Mt. Bachelor, Mt. Jefferson, Mt. Hood, the Sisters mountains, and others. Most of them had snow on top because it had snowed six inches or more two weeks ago. It was really interesting to see Bend and all the beautiful mountains from the top of Pilot Butte.

Before dinner that evening, we went to the downtown area so Steven could return some movies he had borrowed there. We walked upstairs and had a great view of downtown from the picture windows. Steven was checking his phone to see where local restaurants might be and found one about three blocks away. McMenamins was located in the old St. Francis school buildings and had an inside area and a courtyard area with outside heaters. We chose to eat outside, and it was really fun! The waitress asked if we wanted her to light the firepit and we said yes. After that, many more couples and families chose to eat outside too. We saw some children coming outside with towels wrapped around them and found out that there was an indoor pool on the other side of the school building. Their parents were taking them to their car after lessons. We found out that that there was also a soaking pool; one or more secret passageways; and a building with forty hotel rooms, a former convent.

After eating a wonderful meal of Margherita pizza and burgers and fries, we walked back to our car near the library. On the way, a woman sitting in the front courtyard saw Jay's Georgia cap and asked if he was a Georgia graduate. Jay told her he was and so was our daughter, Amy. The woman and her husband had just moved to Bend from Atlanta so that they could be near their son, who'd lived in Bend for a few years. Their son, Joey, told us that he had seen us earlier that day when we were up on Pilot Butte. Steven said he would probably be seeing them around Bend. It was so nice to talk to them. We said goodbye and God bless and then walked the few blocks back to our car.

When we got back to Steven's place, we arranged our luggage and clothes so that we would be ready to leave for California in the morning. Steven was going to drive his car and follow us, so that he could drive back to Oregon in a few days. We would drive south to Bakersfield, California, and then to I-40 and home.

CHAPTER 15

California

On Wednesday, September 27, 2017, we woke up in Bend, Oregon, and got up and packed our cars for our trip to Sacramento, California. I wanted to eat breakfast again at the Victorian Cafe in Bend. So we drove there and had a really nice breakfast. Since there was a lot of food leftover, I asked Steven if we could get a to-go box and take the leftovers back to his place and leave it in the refrig there. He said sure and that he could use the time to check on his business on his computer.

We left for California about 9:00 a.m., and Steven led the way on US 97 in his Pathfinder. We followed in our car all the way through Oregon to California. The drive was beautiful, and we saw signs to Crater Lake. Even though we didn't stop there, we could see beautiful views along the lake area. The temperature had been forty-three degrees when we left Bend but was eighty-five when we stopped for lunch in northern California. It felt really good to me, and I realized why people love the weather there. Even though it was eighty-five degrees, it felt amazing to stand outside and enjoy the sunshine and breeze.

I stood outside and washed our windshield while Jay pumped gas. In Oregon, attendants pump your gas, so Steven wasn't sure if we were supposed to pump our own. But we found out it was okay for us to do that in California.

Across the road, we saw a Mexican restaurant and went inside. An oriental lady said hello to us and said we could sit anywhere. We ordered waters and our food, which she brought to us on a serving cart. We also bought a mexican Coke to bring home with us as a souvenir. Jay says they taste like the original Cokes he had when he was growing up. Steven noticed that there was a Starbucks across the street and wanted to go there to see if they had coffee mugs. He ended up just buying some coffee there.

We continued on to Sacramento through heavy rush hour traffic. After we checked into our hotel, Steven told us he had messaged Michael, a friend formerly from Nashville, who now lived in Sacramento and worked at UC Davis. Michael was going to meet him at a restaurant near our hotel after we had checked in.

We ate at Famous Burger, and then Steven went to meet his friend. When Steven got back to our hotel, two hours later, he said they'd had a good conversation and Michael had said, "Since you're going to San Francisco tomorrow, you have to stop and see the Napa Valley. It's within ten miles of San Francisco."

That was the best idea ever. We went to the Napa Valley for lunch and some shopping at the Napa Running Company. Steven still wears the black and orange Nike running shoes he bought there. We found out later that we were in Napa nine days before the forest fires went through that area in 2017.

Thursday, September 28, 2017, we got up and went to the breakfast room so we could eat before we left for San Francisco. On the television in the breakfast room was the US representative from LA, Steve Scalise. He had been playing at a baseball practice in Washington, DC, in June when a random attacker shot at the people on the field. Steve Scalise was giving a wonderful speech about his recovery and the power of prayer. He thanked his wife and all the first responders who had saved his life. He got a standing ovation from Congress. What a great way to start a wonderful day.

After breakfast, we drove toward San Francisco and stopped for gas in Davis, California.

We saw a Dutch brothers coffee shop across the street and went over there to get coffee for Jay and Steven. We also saw many students walking to class at UC Davis, since we were right next to the campus. It was a beautiful day.

We got back on the road and took the exit to the Napa Valley. We drove several miles and didn't quite know the best place to go there. So we went inside the local CVS and asked the young lady at the front desk for directions. A woman in line said the best place to start was downtown Napa. It was only a mile from where we were, so we drove to downtown and found a good parking space on a main street. We began walking down the sidewalk and saw a sign with several stores and restaurants listed. Then we saw a sign for Napa Running Company to our right. The initials of the store were those of NRC in Nashville, where Steven had worked for several years. There were some shoes on display outside the store and clothes hanging on a rack too. We went inside, and he talked to the girl at the desk. We bought him a Napa Running Company T-shirt. Steven tried on a pair of black Nike running shoes with orange soles that were in the sale bin. The shoes fit him perfectly, and he decided to buy them.

After we left the store, we walked past a small bridge with a beautiful view, and Steven took our picture there. We walked a few more blocks and decided we were hungry enough to eat lunch. We saw a restaurant with the doors open, and the sign said Napa Bistro. So we went inside. It was a beautiful restaurant with pink cloth napkins and white tablecloths. The menus had black and silver covers. The food choices looked amazing!

Steven ordered the lamb burger with sweet potato fries. Jay ordered halibut fish tacos with homemade coleslaw. I ordered the tomato bisque soup with red peppers and croutons and also their homemade focaccia bread. This was my favorite lunch of the whole trip. It was outstanding! Steven and Jay shared some bites of their food with me too, and it was delicious.

After lunch, we walked to the Starbucks a couple of blocks away. Steven bought a few mugs there for his business. Then we went back to our car and drove to San Francisco. I had remembered a scenic overlook right before you cross the Golden Gate Bridge, since I had been there in

1996 for an Abbott work conference. So we took the last exit before the bridge and drove up and around a mountain to the welcome center. We saw some pretty hiking trails there. On our way back over the mountain, we stopped at a scenic parking area and walked down to the nearest flat section with a view of the Golden Gate Bridge in the background. Steven took several selfie pictures of us. It was awesome! It was the first time Jay had been to the West Coast and seen the Pacific Ocean, past the San Francisco Bay.

I thought of Amy, Dillon, Zach, and Matthew, who were in Tokyo, across the Pacific Ocean, and had left for their time there in July. Prayers for them and Godspeed.

We drove over the bay across the Golden Gate Bridge and saw a large boat going under the bridge. Then we drove through San Francisco and parked on Bay Street near the Pier 39 parking garage. We got out and walked a couple of blocks to Pier 39. Before we got to the main pier, we sat down on benches on a dock and watched several large ships and many sailboats nearby. It was 75 degrees and sunny—so beautiful!

We walked to Pier 39 and went into a souvenir shop and bought some postcards and magnets. I also bought a silver trinket box with a picture of the Golden Gate bridge on the top. When we left there, we went to an ice cream shop and bought cones and sat outside and watched the boats for a while. After we finished our cones, I calculated the time it was in Tokyo and thought it might be a good time to call Amy. So we were going to a bench away from the crowds when I felt my phone vibrating in my pocket. It was Amy calling us, so perfect timing. It was a Facetime call, so I held my phone up to show her the boats and the pier.

She told me that Dillon's grandfather, Howie, had passed away at ninety-two years old. Dillon was really sad because Howie had been like a father to him in his teen years. Amy said that Zach and Matthew were a real comfort to him now. She added that they would probably go to Connecticut for a memorial service later. I told her how sorry we were about Howie and that we would pray for them. She said I love you, and so did we. God, comfort their family in this sad time.

After we finished the call, we walked the whole length of the pier. At the end of the pier, we saw about ten sea lions sunning themselves on a dock some fifty feet away below us. We also saw a magician called the Lynx performing on a lower level of the pier. We stood and watched most of the show. He was making jokes and saying "one, two, three" in different languages. He said "uno, dos, tres" in Spanish and "ichi, ban, scratchy" in Japanese. (Amy would think that was funny). We also saw Alcatraz prison off the end of the pier in the bay.

Later it was time to eat dinner before we would drive back to our hotel in Sacramento. We looked at the menu for the Pier 39 market and thought all the seafood looked good, so we were seated in the outdoor area. The host took us to the front courtyard near the outdoor heaters. In San Francisco, the weather gets really cool when the sun goes down, even in summer. I remember buying a sweatshirt in 1996 when I was there in August.

We were waited on by Carlos, and I ordered clam chowder in a bread bowl. Steven ordered the same thing. Jay ordered fish, fries, and slaw. Everything was fresh and delicious. When we left the pier, Steven wanted us to walk to the nearest Starbucks to get some mugs. We walked about four blocks, and Steven bought twenty-two San Francisco mugs. We each carried about four bags for the next few blocks back to our car.

It was about 7:00 p.m. Pacific time and still rush hour when we drove through downtown San Francisco. Steven's Google maps said the best way to go was across the Oakland Bridge. We passed a large building on the right that had a sign, "Opera," and I wondered if it was the same opera house shown in the movie *Pretty Woman*. It sure looked the same. Then we drove over the Oakland Bay Bridge and saw lots of barges with large metal shipping containers on them. Just like the green one that carried Amy's family's furniture to Japan. We also saw cranes that looked like Star Wars figures. So cool! On the way back to Sacramento, we stopped at a Starbucks in Redding, California. Jay bought me a white chocolate mocha coffee because he knew that I liked it. It was so good!

We drove on to our hotel and went right to sleep. It was a really good day—the most wonderful day of our whole trip!

On Friday morning, we got up at 7:30 a.m. and went to breakfast. Then we packed our cars, and Steven said he was going to stop at a Panera to get some of their coffee before he headed north to Oregon. He asked us if we wanted to follow him there. We did because we would be traveling south to Bakersfield, California toward I-40 and then east toward home. Jay and Steven got coffee and pumpkin muffins. I ordered an M&M cookie and some ice water. While there, we talked about Steven's future plans. He told us he was planning on staying in Oregon for this winter so that he could try out some of the winter sports there, and he might come back to Nashville after that.

My prayer when he left Nashville in May was, "Lord, bring him back." We missed him so much, and yet we wanted him to find the path that God has for him. Jeremiah 29:11 says, "I know the plans I have for you says the Lord, plans to prosper you and give you hope and a future." Love and prayers for his present and his future.

We went to our cars and hugged and said goodbye. Steven said, "Only six weeks more until Thanksgiving." Yes we would be waiting for that!

CHAPTER 16

Transition: Buying a House in Oregon, Losing a Grandfather and Registering for UTMB

October, November, December 2017

Only six weeks until we would see Steven again! Between that time, lots of interesting things happened. He got to go to the Bend Oregon music festival weekend in October. His friend, Andi (a girl), from Ashland, Oregon, came to Bend with her boyfriend, Jeremy, and invited Steven to go to some of the movies shown at the festival. Also, her friend Melissa had just moved to Bend and went with them. They had a good time, and Steven made a new friend.

Steven's apartment mate had been contemplating a move downtown, closer to work, for several months. She found a new apartment that she liked and told him she was moving by December 1. That meant Steven had to look for another place to live. He looked at many options—other apartments, houses, RVs, rooms with friends, Airbnbs. The last, seemingly impossible, option was buying another house. What? How could that happen? He said he couldn't really feel good about renting again when he could build equity in a property that he owned.

Our God is a God of the impossible—of making the impossible possible! How great is our God! Help him, Jesus!

When he looked at the real estate listings in and around Bend, he saw a listing about a little A-frame house / cabin in La Pine, Oregon, a town thirty miles south of Bend. Steven said it reminded him of the A-frame house our family stayed in with his Uncle Bobby (Jay's younger brother) and his Aunt Alicia when he was two years old. I said to Steven, "Do you remember being there?"

And Steven said, "Yes, I remember being there and playing upstairs."

"Wow," I said. "Most people's first memories are when they are about three years old or later."

But he said he remembered and has always wanted to own an A-frame house. On Thursday, November 30, 2017, Steven would be closing on his A-frame house in La Pine, Oregon. God bless you and your little (seven hundred-square foot) A-frame!

In the meantime, since the A-frame was uninhabitable (no electricity, water, sewer, and so on), Steven rented an Airbnb in Bend for a few nights and then a room in a house in La Pine for another week. He put all of his other belongings in a storage unit in Bend. While Steven was visiting us for Thanksgiving, he'd purchased a seven-foot-by-seven-foot storage shed from Home Depot, which they held for him at the Home Depot in Bend until he could pick it up. He planned on setting it up on his property in La Pine and staying in it at night, using a sleeping bag and a portable gas generator for heat until he could get his house liveable.

Dear Lord, protect him and keep him safe!

After he got back to Bend on Friday after Thanksgiving, his friend Melissa picked him up at the bus station (he had ridden the bus from the Portland Airport). She took him out to eat, along with two other friends. When she found out about Steven's plans to live in a storage shed during the very cold, snowy Oregon winter, she said he could stay at her place in her extra room. He said he might take her up on her offer one or two days a week. I told him he should do that, especially when bad or stormy weather was predicted. Little did I know that God had different plans.

While Steven was here in Georgia for Thanksgiving, he had shopped in Atlanta, Rome, and Nashville for his online business. My brother, sister, and I moved my ninety-one-year-old dad to a local nursing home in Rome from Florida a few days before Thanksgiving. So we met Steven at the nursing home, and he was able to tell his grandfather (my dad) about his cabin in Oregon and his plans for his business. This happened only a few weeks before my dad passed away and was one of the last lucid conversations he had with anyone before his passing. God's timing was really evident.

Our family had a wonderful Thanksgiving day at our house. Joining us were Jay's brother and sister-in-law, who were home from New Orleans. There too were our nephew Robbie and his wife, Natalie, and their two daughters from Atlanta. Their new daughter, Ryla, was only a few weeks old. She weighed just about six pounds and was absolutely precious. Jay's sister, Kitty, made a birthday cake for Robbie and Steven. So we had great desserts, including pumpkin pie. The only ones missing were Amy, Dillon, Zach, and Matthew, who were in Tokyo. But we got to talk to them on Facetime, so that was good. Zach's favorite dessert is pumpkin pie, and he was saying, "If we were at Mimi's, we would have pumpkin pie!"

I know, Zach. I miss you too!

On Friday morning after Thanksgiving, we left our house at 1:30 a.m. in order to take Steven to the Atlanta Airport. But first Steven ate a huge piece of his birthday cake to tide him over while flying to the West Coast. He arrived back in Bend, Oregon, at 6:00 p.m. PCT, and his friend, Melissa, picked him up at the bus station. They went out to eat, and she asked Steven if he wanted to go anywhere else.

"No thanks," he told her. "I just want to go back to my apartment and sleep."

When he got there, he had to set up an air mattress first, and then he was off to sleep. The next day, he called me and said he had slept twelve hours straight through the night. He said he would be totally moved out by Sunday to the Airbnb in Bend for three nights. After that, he'd head to the room he'd rented in a house in LaPine, near his new house.

On Thursday, November 30, 2017, Steven sent me a picture of him sitting on the front steps of his A-frame house, with a caption that read, "It's official!" and a smiley face.

Congratulations, Steven! That's wonderful! He told me he'd signed the contract for the house on Wednesday and then gotten a check from the bank and paid for it on Thursday. So he had officially become the owner of his A-frame on Thursday.

In the picture he sent of the front of the cabin, I saw a small pine tree right in front of the main door. Steven said he needed to decorate it for the holidays. And in a couple of hours, he sent me another picture, this time with a garland on his little pine tree. He'd gone to a local store and bought some decorations for it. The little tree looks really festive!

Also, it was no coincidence that I'd seen *A Charlie Brown Christmas* on TV last night. Charlie Brown gets a pine tree for the Christmas play, and everyone makes fun of it for being small and scraggly. But then, after several children borrow some decorations from Snoopy's doghouse and decorate the tree, they sing Christmas carols around it. Linus recites the entire biblical Christmas story from Luke chapter 2:

And she brought forth her firstborn son,
and wrapped him in swaddling clothes, and
laid him in a manger, because there was no
room for them in the inn …

For unto you is born this day in the city of
David a Saviour, which is Christ the Lord."

Hallelujah!

On Friday, December 1, 2017, Jay and I went to visit my dad in the Rome nursing home. He seemed much better and more alert than he has been. We brought him a vanilla milkshake from McDonalds, and he drank some of it. He also wanted a Coke. So I asked his nurse if he could have that. She said yes and brought him a canned Coke. My dad drank most all of it! Then I trimmed his hair in the back and sides, using scissors I'd brought from home. He looked so much better. I gathered up his laundry in a bag and told him I would take it home and wash it and bring it back soon. We said goodbye and told him, "I love you."

On the way home, Steven called us and said he hadn't had to work on Friday so he'd eaten breakfast in La Pine. "I have a new breakfast place," he told us, adding that he'd had biscuits and gravy and that the people there had been very friendly. The weather in Oregon was in the forties, which was mild for December. God help Steven each day!

The next time we heard from him was on December 5, when he called and told us he'd stayed at an Airbnb in Bend for three nights and had now moved closer to his house in La Pine. He was now staying at an Airbnb at a house in LaPine, owned by a nice woman named Linda. Steven said she had made coffee for him every morning. One morning, she was making French toast and asked if he wanted some. "Sure," he said.

She also found out from him that he was going to try and live in a storage shed while he worked on his new property. She told him that the winters in Oregon were really brutal, and he should look into something else. So he went and talked to an RV dealer and was able to buy a new 2018 RV. At eighteen feet long, his RV has a full-sized bed and a stove, microwave, and refrig. He was able to tow it with his Pathfinder and got it placed on his property on Thursday. He sent us some pictures.

Friday night was his first night staying in the RV. I texted him on Saturday and asked how it went. The heater hadn't worked, so he'd slept in his sleeping bag. He was going to go to Bend to the RV dealer and get some help so that he would have heat for the weekend. Dear Lord, help Steven to have heat tonight! Watch over him at his new place! Thank you for Linda and her suggestion that he have a better place to stay while he renovates his A -rame!

Jeremiah 20:11 says, "I know the plans I have for you says the Lord. Plans to prosper you and not to harm you, to give you hope and a future." I claim this verse for him in the name of Jesus our Lord. I love you, Steven.

***

On Friday, December 8, 2017, around 4:00 a.m., Jay had looked outside our house in Georgia and said, "It's snowing!"

I got up and went to the picture window in our dining room and saw a beautiful continuous snowfall. Jay checked the local news on his computer tablet, and it showed that all the schools were closed. Yay, it was a snow day!

When Amy and Dillon were transferred to Tokyo in July 2017 and they and Zach and Matthew had made the move, they'd asked us to keep their kitty, Chubbs, for six months, while she went through a quarantine period before she could be admitted to Japan. We said yes and had enjoyed having her with us. Her favorite place in our house was the screened porch. So, when she went out on the porch that morning, she didn't know what to think about the "white stuff" falling from the sky. The kitty wanted to come back inside because it was cold. Later in the day, she went back outside and stayed longer. By the time it stopped snowing, we had a measurable six inches of snow.

The next day, the roads were cleared, and we decided to go to Rome, Georgia, to see my dad at the nursing home and Jay's sister, Kitty, at her house. When I walked into my dad's room, I noticed an immediate change in his appearance. He was sitting up in bed, but when I said, "Good morning, Daddy," he didn't respond or open his eyes. I went right away to the nurse's station and asked the charge nurse about his condition. He said a nurse practitioner had been called and had ordered antibiotics after discovering he had another UTI (urinary tract infection). I went back to his room and sat with him for awhile; still no response.

A nurse named Zach came into the room and said he was going to start an IV so that they could give him the antibiotics. I told him that my dad was right-handed and that it was best if he could start the IV in his left hand. Probably the last movement that I saw my dad make was to lift his left hand. When he did that, I knew he was asking me what was happening, because he wasn't able to speak.

So I told him, "Daddy, they are going to start an IV to give you medicine for your infection."

He opened his eyelids, but his eyes were glazed over, and I knew he couldn't see me. Then I noticed that his breathing was labored. When I told his nurse about it, he said he would check on him and call me soon.

Jay and I said goodbye to Daddy and then left to go to Jay's sister's house. On the way, I messaged my brother, Joel, and told him about our dad's condition. He called me back a little while later and said he had gone to the nursing home after I'd called. My brother said my dad was much worse than he had been the previous day and asked the hospice nurse, who had been called in, what could be done for him. After talking over the options, Joel and I both decided to tell the nurse to make him comfortable. She said she would stay with him that night. We finished our dinner with Jay's sister, and Joel called to tell me that the hospice nurse had given my dad some medication and that he was breathing easier now and peaceful. Joel knew this nurse from his visits to Rome nursing homes through his ministry at FBC Rome. He said she was very nice.

The next morning, Sunday, Jay and I got ready to go to the nursing home to see my dad. First I talked to my brother. He told me the nurse had called; our dad had passed away during the night. Joel had taken care of the initial arrangements and said we didn't need to go there. It was heartbreaking. But though I was very I said, I took comfort in knowing that we'd been there and talked to my dad yesterday and had called in help for him.

I called Amy and she said to let her know about the funeral arrangements; she might be able to arrange to be here earlier than her previously arranged flight for Christmas. Then I called Steven and told him about Papa Joe (that's what the grandchildren called my dad). He told me how sorry he was, and I told him it was very good that he'd been able to visit with my dad during Thanksgiving. They'd been able to have a really good conversation. Most of what I heard Steven say to him was that he was working for a shipping company and trying to buy a house he could renovate and then live in. I didn't hear my dad's response, but he seemed to be positive about it. This was Steven's last conversation with his grandfather, and I'm so glad that it was good!

Steven wasn't able to travel back for the funeral, as he had to work. I was so glad he'd been here for Thanksgiving and that we would see him soon for Christmas when he would fly into Charlotte, North Carolina, on Christmas Eve.

Thank you, Lord, for Steven's life and for my dad's life. God is faithful and has been faithful in the past. Help Steven in his future!

My dad had two funeral services, the first one locally in Rome, Georgia, at Joel's church, First Baptist of Rome. The second was a military graveside service in Sarasota, Florida, at the Sarasota National Cemetery. Amy was due to fly home from Japan for Christmas on December 21. Dillon had his office try for three days to change her flight to December 17, with her flying into Tampa so that we could pick her up and take her to Sarasota with us. That way, we could attend my dad's service there together. When she called on December 12 to tell me that she had a flight to Tampa on December 18, I cried. I told her we were so glad she would be with us there!

Amy emailed me her new flight schedule, and I noticed that the travel agent addressed Dillon as Dillon-san and Amy as Amy-san, a Japanese courtesy. So, when I received the flight information, I messaged her back and said, "Thank you for the flight information, Amy-san. I love you."

Amy replied back to me, "I love you too, Mama-san."

So very precious!

On Monday, December 18, we drove to Tampa and picked Amy up near the airport. It was good to see her again, after six months of her and her family being in Tokyo. Then Jay, Amy, and I continued on to Sarasota. We stayed at the local Holiday Inn-Lakewood, where we had been many times before. Joel and Cherry were also staying there, so we got together and went to a local mall. We ate dinner together at California Pizza Kitchen. It was a time of sharing old memories and talking together.

On Tuesday, December 19, we were to be at the cemetery by 10:30 a.m. We left the hotel at 9:30, and the weather was seventy-five degrees and sunny. Since we got there early for the service, a volunteer told us we could drive around the cemetery to the left and view some of the beautiful glass structures there; one looked like huge wings. All of the graves had pine wreaths with red bows. It was a beautiful sight. Then we went to the right to get in line for the procession.

When we got out of our car, I saw several navy officers and other military officers in full dress uniform. A young lady naval officer in white approached me, since I am the oldest child in our family. "How are you today, ma'am?" she asked.

I said I was doing well and asked her how she was. She

said it was an honor to escort me today. I put my right arm through her left arm, and we walked to the bench in front of the casket. I told her thank you. Then Amy came to sit on my left, and Jay sat to the left of her.

Two sailors in white dress uniforms took the American flag off of my dad's casket. They folded it in half and then in half again. Then they folded it in triangles until it was one perfect triangle. One of the young sailors took the flag in his arms and stood in front of me. "On behalf of the president of the United States and the US Navy, we honor his service," he said. Then he handed me the flag, took off his right glove, turned back toward me, and knelt right in front of me. Of course, by that time, I had tears streaming down my face. Then, looking directly into my eyes, the sailor said, "Thank you for your father's service to our country. Thank you for letting us be a part of this today. It is an honor to be here."

I looked at him and said, "Thank you. God bless you in everything you do."

Later, on the way back to our hotel, Jay said that, when the sailor took off his glove, it was a sign to the other sailors that what happened next was to be "off script." I had chills all over when it happened. What a wonderful ceremony!

God bless all those in our military, past and present!

We did go to Charlotte, North Carolina, for Christmas and had a wonderful time with our family and staying with Amy and Dillon's friends. After we'd said goodbye to Amy, Dillon, Zach, and Matthew (they would be flying back to Tokyo from Charlotte), Steven rode back to Georgia with us. We had several days together, and he was also able to meet friends in Nashville. His flight back to Oregon was on January 3, 2018.

As we were taking him to the Atlanta Airport on that day, Steven was checking his phone. He looked up and said, "You know, today is the last day to register for the UTMB in Mont Blanc."

I asked him if he had registered.

"I thought it would be too costly so I haven't registered," he replied.

"Oh please go ahead and register today, and we'll give you the entrance fee," I told him.

It turned out to be $319, which wasn't too bad. I just didn't want him to miss the deadline and regret it later.

The UTMB had been his goal and his dream for several years. To qualify, a person had to complete at least three designated races in the United States and finish within an allotted time period. He had completed the Bear 100 in Utah/Idaho in 2014, the Bryce Canyon 100 in 2015 in Utah, and the Olallie Mountain Lakes 100 in 2017 in Oregon— not to mention several other qualifying races in Colorado, Arizona, Utah, Idaho, and Wisconsin. We couldn't give up on his dream.

CHAPTER 17

Preplanning our Trip to the UTMB and Unconventional UTMB Training

After Steven registered for the UTMB, plans started rolling. It seemed like all we needed was faith and belief that this was going to happen. God took care of the rest.

By mid-January, Steven had already booked his flight to Chamonix, France, and his room in a chalet there. One of his friends, a runner who'd raced in the UTMB before, suggested the chalet and told him what stores might be helpful for supplies while he was in France. He sent us pictures of the chalet—showing a full view of the Swiss Alps and Mont Blanc. It looked amazing ! (And when we were there, we'd find it to be exactly like the pictures—only better because it was live.)

Jay and I booked our passage on Cunard Lines, the *Queen Mary II*, from New York City to Southampton, England, and also trains to Paris and Chamonix, France, through a travel agent in Nashville named Sherry. She was a wonderful help to us. We wanted to be in Chamonix within twenty-four hours of Steven completing the race, and we were!

Dear Lord, help us with our plans. Protect Steven and help him to finish the race and feel good about it.

Unconventional UTMB Training by Steven McNeal August 26, 2018

I'm not sure what a "conventional" training routine for Europe's famed UTMB 100-miler would be, but I'm pretty sure my training has been decidedly unconventional. UTMB, short for Ultra-Trail du Mont-Blanc, is a 170K (105.6-mile) trail running event that circumnavigates the tallest mountain in Europe west of Russia; takes place on a trail that goes through three countries (France, Italy, and Switzerland); and has about 2,300 participants, who have prepared and entered through a complex qualification and lottery system. This has been my dream race and, after three years of being qualified and entering the lottery, I finally made it into the event for 2018!

For any of you reading who are mostly interested in my training numbers for the event, let me give a brief overview of my training to this point. Then I'll rewind into the nuts and bolts of my routines. In summary, I started focusing on UTMB around January 2018, when my weekly mileage was around 30 miles per week or so. From there, I did a gradual buildup of mileage, with my focal point being hitting weekly mileage goals. I worked up to a peak of 70 miles per week with a little over ten thousand feet of gain at an average altitude of around five thousand feet, with about 80 to 90 percent of my miles being on trails mixing lots of hiking and supereasy-paced running. Almost all of my training took place in Central Oregon, where I live and have access to some amazingly diverse and beautiful landscapes in the Cascade mountain range. My miles were a little on the low end for an undertaking as big as the UTMB. But that's where the rest of my story comes into play.

I almost didn't even capitalize on my successful UTMB entry for 2018. Last fall, I stretched myself financially to the limit with a purchase of an A-frame cabin in Oregon. With a low-paying, self-employed job, I shouldn't have been able to secure financing on a distressed property that needed a ton of work. But with the tenacity of an ultrarunner, I did not give up, and I landed ownership of a cabin that hasn't been occupied in over a decade and has no utilities. I had no real financing plan for the renovations other than digging into credit card debt, so I was really taking a leap of faith with the property purchase. When I got into UTMB, it wasn't exactly a venture that fit well into my overly strained annual budget for 2018. I decided I wouldn't think about my budget or any rational financial decisions, and I decided to ignore the prudent internal financial alarms going off when I added a flight to Europe, an apartment in France, and other travel expenses to an overextended budget.

So after winning the UTMB lottery and again rolling the dice with my financial future, I decided I'd better get myself to training. Now, the training needed for a 100-miler in the Alps is enough to cause a typical human a lot of inconvenience, with the trimming of hours upon hours of Netflix marathons to make time for hitting the mountain trails to prepare one's body for the trial ahead. I like Netflix as much as the next person, but currently do not have it. But I have had an overflowing schedule, with managing my online business to pay the bills and a massive renovation project on the A-frame. Most of my summer days were spent meeting early with my two contractors, jumping in to help them some, and stepping away to work on my online business to try to be able to pay off everyone. So adding on UTMB training has been a challenge in finding time and energy and trying to strike a balance with all of it.

Oh, and did I mention that I'm living in an RV and dry camping in the midst of all this? I bought a new eighteen-foot travel trailer back in November 2017 after I bought my cabin, so that I could have something to live in while rehabilitating the property. And, no joke, as soon as I towed the new RV to my property, my personal vehicle's transmission went out. Long story short, with a tight budget, I decided to get a smaller vehicle that could no longer tow the RV. And with no working utilities (no water!) at my property, that meant I needed to dry camp. This means I kept my RV winterized and with no running water. I bring in all my own water, mostly wash dishes by leaning outside the RV door, and bathroom privileges are not privileges. I won't go there, but it's not a fun long-term situation. It gives me all the more motivation to get the A-frame ready for me to move in. But it's a big project and is hard to push along without big dollars paving the way.

With all this happening at the same time in my life, I

have had to come up with a somewhat modified strategy for training. I still decided to focus on the weekly mileage goals because that has worked for me in the past, and it's mentally the way to go for me to feel like I'm making progress. But I had also decided that I would do two-week buildups in mileage, followed by a recovery week. It was a lot more palatable for me to only face two weeks of training before getting a break, rather than longer cycles I have done before—like three weeks up, one week down. For my recovery weeks, I normally would focus on cutting back a certain percentage, like going from a buildup to 50 miles in a week down to a recovery of 25 to 30 miles the following week. However, with everything zapping my time and energy, I decided that my recovery weeks could be as little as I wanted—which sometimes ended up being only 5-10 miles in a recovery week. I was able to get in some bigger runs on weekends especially, notably on the PCT, up Marion Peak (the biggest peak between Mt. Bachelor and Diamond Peak in Oregon), Broken Top, and up on St. Helens in Washington state.

Let's talk nutrition just briefly, because I feel like it plays a bigger role than I realized when I first started doing ultras. Back when I started training in January, I was eating a lot of McDonalds. Yes, that place with the arches. This is because I was saving every dime I could tooth and nail, and Mickey D's was the cheapest place to get decent coffee. And they have some killer deals on their app for food coupons. I also didn't have internet on my property for a while, so McDonalds really helped me get through the bitter Central Oregon winter with their free Wi-Fi and warm coffee. However, I knew that, as UTMB approached, I needed to make some dietary changes. I gradually switched back to a higher-fat diet that I'd used to help me at my last 100-mile race, the Mountain Lakes 100 in 2017. I believe the diet really helped teach my body to use fat for fuel, delaying any potential bonks.

It worked like a charm at ML100, so I've done my best to gear my eating the same way this time, although I haven't been as strict. So we'll see how it plays out!

All in all, I feel like I'm at a major turning point in my life through this whole experience. I found that, as I was training, I really started to dread the buildup weeks and look forward to and savor the recovery weeks. Training has already started to feel like a grind throughout this process, and the only thing keeping me going is that I want to and have to fulfill this dream of running UTMB. I'm excited to fly into Switzerland next week, make my way to Chamonix, and prepare for the run of my life around Mt. Blanc. I'm going to soak it all in, stay within myself as much as I can, and then grind out what I can when the going gets tough. And then, after UTMB, I'll meet up with my wonderful parents, who are literally cruising across the Atlantic on a ship called the *Queen Mary II*, and we're going to eat and tour our way through as much of Europe as we can! When I finally return to the States and solitude of my RV, that A-frame better get ready for some serious business, because it will be a new life with ultrarunning dreams lived and A-frame visions to live out.

CHAPTER 18

UTMB, France: Our Voyage There and Back (with a 100-Mile Race in between)

August 23–September 25, 2018

On August 23, Jay and I left our home in Summerville, Georgia, and drove north toward New York City, where we would board our ship, *the Queen Mary II*, for a transatlantic trip across to Southampton, England. Then we were scheduled for a series of train rides across England and France to the eastern side of France in Chamonix. We hoped to be there in Chamonix a few hours after Steven would be finished running the UTMB.

Our trip to New York City went very well. Our first day, we drove to Salem, Virginia (near Vermont and Blacksburg, Virginia) and ate dinner near our hotel at a place called Billy's Barn. They had an extensive menu, with Mexican dishes, American hamburgers and steaks, and more. Jay had a mushroom/swiss burger, and I had a steak salad. Both were delicious. The next day, we drove to Allentown, Pennsylvania and saw a classic car convention, with many of the cars being in our hotel parking lot. Then on Saturday, we drove to Brooklyn, New York, and our hotel for the night before we were to board the ship. After we arrived at our hotel, we asked the Oriental girl at the front desk where to park our car. She told us that we could park under the bridge right across the street. So we moved our car under the Verrazano Bridge and prayed that we would still have tires by morning.

The next morning, Sunday, we walked outside and checked on our car. There were many more cars parked under the bridge than had been there yesterday, but our car was fine. We ate breakfast at our hotel. Then we checked out and got in our car and drove to the Brooklyn Terminal, where we saw the *Queen Mary II* ship for the first time. It looked so large! We parked our car in the long-term parking lot there and took several pictures of the *Queen Mary II* and the Statue of Liberty. Jay had been on the *Queen Elizabeth II* in 1970, when he sailed home from England that summer. His sighting of the Statue of Liberty when that ship was entering New York Harbor was one of his best memories of coming back home.

After we got our luggage out of our car, we carried our bags up to the front entrance of the terminal, where lots of people were congregating. A porter was telling us to load our main luggage onto carts, since we already had the official luggage tags on the handles. Then we went inside the terminal and got in line to go through security. There, security guards checked our passports and IDs and gave us our boarding passes for the voyage to Southampton. Then we went to a waiting area, where hundreds of other passengers were waiting. We met several nice people, including a couple who were going to Monkey World to see their seven-year-old grandson and a young man named Graham, who was going to travel to Belgium and Italy also.

We got to our stateroom and met our steward, Chris, who was from the Philippines. Later, I found out that Cunard Lines goes to the Philippines to recruit people to work for the company. Amy had told me that her au pair in Tokyo, Mae-Lin, was from the Philippines and thah she sent most of her pay back home to her family. It was really amazing to know how connected people could be. In our stateroom was a ship's newsletter that told us of the day's events and a free bottle of sparkling cider from the captain. We looked at each other and said, "That's probably the only thing that's free on this cruise."

While we were just starting our cruise, Steven was preparing to fly to France for his UTMB race in a few days. He had to bring eighteen specific items to place in his pack for the race—among them rainproof pants, gloves, and a bandage. He had to get insurance in case he was stranded on a mountain or was injured during the race. I was praying for him every few hours now.

Our first night's dinner was in the Britannia dining room, and we were seated with a lovely couple from England. The food was very good—beef with mushroom gravy and ice cream and sorbet for dessert. We talked for a couple of hours and told our new friends about our family and about Steven's race. Later, several people would ask us how Steven was doing—after he had begun running. It meant a lot to have them interested about him.

For breakfast, we went to the Britannia dining room again and were seated with several couples—some from England; one from Calgary, Canada; and another from Minneapolis. The couple from England were Caroline and Allen. We saw Caroline after breakfast, and she had purchased an art kit and was going to take the watercolor art class. I planned on taking a similar class when we came back from France.

After walking around the ship's deck and sitting on deck chairs for a while, we went to a lecture given by one of the descendants of John Jacob Astor, named Lord Astor of Hever. He made a joke that one of the men who introduced him at a recent conference made a mistake and called him "Lord Astor of Heaven." He said he could only wish. British humor is so subtle. He also talked about his family, past and present. He had a wife and four daughters and one son. He lived on a farm in Hever and showed a picture of the farm, which was beautiful! His great-uncle John Jacob Astor and his nineteen-year-old pregnant wife were on that ill-fated voyage of the *Titanic* in 1912. She was rescued by the ship *Carpathia* and later had their son, William.

For lunch, we went to the King's Grill and selected food from a marvelous buffet. We sat near a young man who had a frame that reminded us of Steven, tall and slender. Later, we learned his name was Nick, and his wife, Janice, also sat with us. She was from Scotland and, it turneds out, they ere moving from England to Scotland on Friday after they got off the ship. Nick was in the Royal Navy and had been for twenty-seven years. He told us he only had eight years until retirement. He ran in a charity race last year, similar to Mont Blanc; only it was three days of 100-miles a day, and they spent the nights in tents. In order to find a house in Scotland, Janice sent her mom and dad a picture of a house that she thought was interesting. Her parents went to see the house and told her that it was in good shape. So they purchased the house and were moving there next week.

Janice told us many useful facts about touring in Paris, since they'd been several times. Notre-Dame cathedral was free to visitors, she told us, but if we wanted to climb to the top, we would have to paid a fee. She advised that, if we wanetd to eat at a restaurant, we should go a few blocks from the main Champs Élysées to find a cheaper meal. Plus, she told us about tour buses in Paris that allowed yout to get on and off to see the sights. (We used the hop-on hop off buses in Paris and London; some people call them the ho-hos.)

Janice and Nick were such a lovely couple, and we wished them good luck and God bless!

I also got a call from my sister's husband, my brother-in-law, Stanley, from Atlanta. He was calling to see how we were doing on board the ship. I told him all was going well and that we really enjoyed the food and the conversations with different people. Stanley said Steven was probably flying over our ship today, since he was flying to Amsterdam and then on to France the next day. That was so true.

So much of our trip was in tandem with Steven's agenda. He would begin his race in a couple of days. God help him and all the runners.

The next day, Steven had arrived in Chamonix, France. He sent us a picture of the view of Mont Blanc behind his apartment there. When Jay saw the picture, he said, "The hills are alive," meaning it reminded him of the view in the movie *Sound of Music* with Julie Andrews. There was a large snowcapped mountain with green grass at the foot of the mountain, which appeared to be right in his backyard. So beautiful! God help him tomorrow!

The next day was Friday, August 31, 2018, UTMB Race start day! We ate breakfast in the Britannia dining room with a few British couples and an American couple at our table. Irene and Bill were from Asheville, North Carolina, and were meeting their daughter and going sightseeing. They had been to Paris before and gave us information about speaking the language—*merci* for thank you and *s'il vous plait* for please, *Madame* for Mrs. And *Monsieur* for Mr., *bonjour* for hello and *bonsoir* for good evening. Irene said that any attempt to speak French there would be appreciated.

I had been studying French on my Duolingo app on my phone and was also refreshing myself since I had taken French classes in high school fifty years ago. Irene that there were several good restaurants and snack shops in St. Pancras train station, where we would go to board the Eurostar train for Paris. Later my French lessons would really make a difference when we arrived in Paris and met our chauffeur to our first hotel.

That afternoon, we went to a piano recital given by Ray Lemond on the works of Puccini. He said that Puccini had decided to write opera music when he was thirteen years old, and he never stopped. It was so interesting.

Steven had begun his race, and we would follow him on the UTMB Live app. The race officially began at 6:00 p.m. France time. We were about two hours behind his time and had to rely on weak internet signals on board the ship. Amy was tracking the race on her computer in Tokyo, so we had help from different points in the world. Just having to login any time we wanted to receive a text or check on the app info seemed to take a long timel. It was slow going!

At dinner, I wore my hot pink dress and pink wrap. Our waiter said I looked beautiful. And a nice lady took our picture before we went into the dining room and said we looked really good. We'd so enjoyed our dinners there!

After dinner, we went upstairs to check on Steven's progress in his race. Through the livestreaming on the app, we were able to see him go through the checkpoint at mile 23, and he texted us when he was at mile 25 and said he felt good. God bless him!

On Saturday, due to excellent coverage on the UTMB Live app, I had gotten up at 4:00 a.m. ship time (6:00 a.m. Chamonix time) and got online. And I was able to see a video of Steven going through another checkpoint, Courmayeur, Italy, at 71 kilometers. This was his favorite checkpoint during the race because the local people made it seem like they were family and cheered him on. In the video, he was doing well and among a group of at least three others. I prayed that he would have people around him during the race. God help him!

After seeing this video, I texted Amy Steven's current info and his bib number, which was 1960. She had been checking on his progress on the website and praying for him too. Thanks, Amy, my prayer warrior daughter!

We ate breakfast at the Britannia dining room and then walked around the ship. We sat by a window on Deck 2 and soon saw several pods of dolphins alongside the ship.

Most were in groups of two or three. Jay saw two dolphins very close to our window. We called out to some of the other guests near us that there were dolphins, and several of the children saw the dolphins out their windows. It was so exciting!

We had a great lunch at the King's Court buffet. Then we went to a lecture on Michelangelo given by an Italian artist. He said that Michelangelo had a few disagreements with Pope Julius II when he was painting the Sistine Chapel—the room in the Vatican built to the exact dimensions of Solomon's temple as recorded in the Bible. So Michelangelo painted one of the figures with the face of Pope Julius. Also we learned that Michelangelo carved the *Pietà*, of Mary holding her son Jesus, out of one piece of marble in 1499 when he was nineteen or twenty years old. Another artist claimed that Michelangelo did not carve this piece, but Michelangelo carved his own name on a secret place of the *Pietà* to prove he had been the artist. It was so interesting—intrigue in the fifteenth century.

That evening, we ate our last dinner of our voyage in the Britannia dining room. We really enjoyed our dinners there, and we liked our waiters very much. They were so nice and helpful. They asked us if we would be back, and we told them we would return in two weeks for the trip back to New York.

On our way back to our room for the night, we rode on an elevator with an Irish man and his wife—a couple we had met at dinner. They were going back to Ireland to see their dog. We told them our son was still running in his race. He looked us in the eye and said he hoped our son did well. Then another gentleman in the elevator asked where our son was running. We told him that he was in the UTMB in Chamonix, France. This man said his son-in-law was one of the people who planped these races. I told him that his son-in-law did a good job because we were able to see personal videos of Steven at many of the checkpoints and villages along the race course.

That coverage had been a real comfort to us. We bought thirty more minutes of Wi-Fi so we could check on Steven's progress through his second night on the course.

By the time it was our morning around 8:01 a.m., Steven was passing through Triente (about 140 kilometers in). He only had 31 kilometers to go. God help him to finish!

My phone had a message from Verizon: "Welcome to Great Britain. You have 100 texts and 100 minutes of data." (We had purchased an international package.) That was a welcome sight! Jay and I ate breakfast in the King's Court so that we could sit at a table with large windows and see our ship pulling into Southampton, England, at sunrise. It was incredibly beautiful!

At Southampton, we disembarked at the Queen Elizabeth Cruise terminal and got on a large bus to St. Pancras train station in London. Our bus driver told us it would take about two hours to get there and explained what to do in case of an emergency. But he said we probably wouldn't have any emergencies since he was driving.

At St. Pancras, we found a French shop in the food court called Patisserie Valerie, and we ordered a large ham and cheese sandwich on French bread to share. The shop girl asked us if we wanted it hot, and we said, "Yes." Then she heated it in a panini grill and served us. It was so delicious and our first taste of real French cuisine.

Then it was time to go to the part of the station where we would board the Eurostar high-speed train to Paris. We placed our luggage in bins and went through security, and I spoke my first French words to the French police who examined our passports and then stamped them. I said, "Merci, Monsieur," and they just gave me a look and nodded. Oh well. I guess smiling wasn't part of their protocol.

We boarded our car of the train and were helped by a really nice steward, who helped us place our luggage in racks near the doors. Then came the best part of our trip—at 14:22 p.m., after we got to our seats and my phone picked up the Wi-Fi on the train, and I started receiving texts. The first message was from Amy in Tokyo telling us that Steven had just finished his race! Hallelujah!

The total distance of the race was 171 kilometers. Steven said that his GPS watch read 116 miles at the finish line. Wow! We were so happy he finished and that he could now rest and eat good food and enjoy the rest of his trip. Praise be to God for seeing him through the last few days. And praise be for his friends who prayed and for the ones who came to Chamonix to cheer him on—Melissa, Emma, and Joanna. Thank you, God, and bless them too.

CHAPTER 19

UTMB at Last

UTMB: A Blanc Canvas by Steven McNeal
July 2019

When I started running in 1999, it felt like a way to have goals to strive for, PRs (personal records) to chase, and a way to measure progress while pursuing higher levels of fitness. Over time, these pursuits remained, but running also became about connecting in a community of like-minded people and bonding more with the earth and natural surroundings through trail running. That naturally led to ultrarunning and the continual "addiction" led me to my holy grail of running, UTMB. After three years of trying, this year I finally got to run in the 2018 Ultra-Trail du Mont-Blanc.

If you're interested in my preparation for the event, you can read my previous post [in Chapter 17]. Here I want to go into some details of the race itself. Let me give some quick pre-event details first. UTMB is a circumnavigation of Mont Blanc, starting and ending in Chamonix, France. I traveled from Oregon and ultimately arrived in France a little over forty-eight hours before the UTMB start. I had just enough time to settle into my apartment and hang with my friends from Oregon, Melissa and Emma, who came from overseas to visit and watch my start. The night before the race, I magically slept for fourteen hours and woke up at 2:00 p.m., waking four hours before the 6:00 p.m. start! Not a bad way to begin a journey of 170 kilometers.

The afternoon of our start brought cool air and a steady cold drizzle of rain. I lined up in the quaint streets of Chamonix with more than two thousand other trail runners from around the world with the same dream. A fog above moved across the towering mountain peaks, hinting at our trials to come. The announcers commented that the weather was similar to the inaugural UTMB running. A helicopter involved in race happenings hovered down and held steady in the fog. Birds were flying hurriedly overhead, seeming to sense the extra energy in the air. Vangelis' "Conquest of Paradise" played through the sound system, while you could see the steely looks of determination on the race favorites faces on the projector screen.

It was, hands down, the most epic start to any race I have experienced.

After the starting gun went off, we funneled through the streets of Chamonix for the first mile or so. Since I started in the back, we were walking for the first ten minutes or so with the tightness of thousands of runners bottlenecking through the streets lined with enthusiastic spectators. Finally we spread out enough to break out into a jogging rhythm and, shortly thereafter, hit the trail.

The first five or six miles were gently rolling, as I'd expected from the race profile. Then the first of many big climbs commenced. Since my legs were fresh, I don't have a ton of memories of this uneventful climb, but the way down is still etched in my memory. Since the race start was at 6:00 p.m., by the time I was going down this first long descent, it was fairly dark already. It was a steep grade downward, making it difficult to decide whether to run or hike down the uneven, slick grass and mud mixture. I saw at least one person fall while going down, and I wouldn't have been surprised if I followed suit. Fortunately, I managed to navigate down to the first major aid station uneventfully and was rewarded with a vast variety of food and drink options.

My eyes honed in on the cheese, meat, and chocolate. And since I had prepared for the race on a high-fat diet, it was all fair game for my stomach. So I went for it.

The rest of the first night for me involved steady movement, with a slow hike uphill for a few hours up a rockier climb in a train of a thousand. We were all generally held to the slowest person's pace in front of us, as it was difficult to pass uphill on the rocky terrain. I could occasionally sense impatience behind me, and some would exert great effort to pass a few people when the trail widened slightly, or they would take extreme side options off trail. I took the approach of conserving energy and just being content with the pace set above me.

Finally, day two broke, and I had moved from France to Italy. One thing I will note here is that, throughout the race, I felt more connected to the bystanders than I did with the fellow runners, which was very different from races I have done in the States. Most of the time during UTMB when you passed fellow runners, neither of you knew if you even spoke the same language, so the common protocol while passing was not to say anything. The spectators, on the other hand, were some of the most engaging that I have ever seen. Most people on the sidelines would cheer each person on, at least with clapping, and more commonly words of encouragement, often noting your name since it was on each of our race bibs. When running through France, the encouragement I often received was, "Allez, allez, Steven" (Go, go, Steven). In Italy, it switched to, "Bravo, Steven." I also high-fived so many kids throughout the whole course, and their excitement was infectious. I loved it.

My favorite memory of this first day in Italy was coming

into and going through Courmayeur, a classically scenic town with cobblestone streets nestled in a surrounding of towering mountain peaks. Cormayuer also has a major aid station for UTMB in a large gymnasium, and it was considered the unofficial halfway point, although it was a little short of halfway in overall distance. This was a good venue for me to find a spot in the corner with a chair, kick off my shoes, and let my tired body rest for a quick spell. I really took my time here and savored being close to the halfway point. Eventually, I got my immediate needs taken care of and gradually made my way through the rest of the town and started heading up the trails scaling one of the nearby peaks.

As day two wore on, I was finally starting to feel the need to take a nap, since it had been over twenty-four hours since I'd slept in Chamonix. I remember thinking how nice it was going to be when I got to the next aid station and could lay down and rest for a bit. This marked the beginning of the lowest point for me during the event. When I finally arrived at this ray-of-hope station, I found out that I only had twenty minutes before the time cutoff, and the lady checking me in informed me that I needed to change into my waterproof pants due to conditions ahead. Since I had to eat, use the bathroom, and change my pants, there would be no time for this much-needed nap I had been craving. As I was going through the production of taking off my pack to find my wate-proof pants (part of my mandatory gear), I remember squatting down and feeling my legs just shaking with fatigue. I still had 50 miles through the Alps to go, with a night section right in front of me and no time to rest. It almost brought me to tears, and I definitely toyed with the thought of throwing in the towel at this point. Ultimately, I decided to quiet the voices of concern, man up, and continue on the journey.

From there, it was an upward climb in the fast-approaching dark, up toward Grand Col Ferret—the peak where Italy ends and Switzerland begins. As I went ever so slowly up this climb, I passed multiple people throwing up on the side of the trail, like we were in the midst of battle together. It was getting quite windy and cold out at this high elevation, and I was still desperately craving sleep. After hours of climbing, I could see men in thick orange parka jackets at the top of Grand Col Ferret, with a lighted tent next to them. My confused mind wanted that tent to be an aid station. However, when I reached the men, they merely checked my bib and waved me along. No rest for the weary here.

As I started the descent into Switzerland, my back was starting to feel fatigued from wearing my pack for so long. I couldn't jog down without it feeling like my lower back could seize up at any given moment. I knew I had left the previous aid station within minutes of the time cutoff and I didn't have time to spare. But I was so weary. I had to shift my thoughts to what I needed to do to survive. It wasn't about the event at this point. I thought to myself, *If I just needed to simply survive getting myself miles and miles through this terrain right now, what would I need to do?* It was clear to me that the answer to that question was to rest. So right then and there on the side of that mountain in the dark, I took off my pack and used it as a pillow on the side of the trail in the tall flowing grass. I could feel my body decompress and release stress as I lay there, knowing my UTMB dream could be coming to an end soon due to timing out. I heard a few passing runners checking on me and realizing I was just resting. After about fifteen minutes had passed without any true sleep but some much needed rest, I geared back up and got back to moving.

Somehow, my body took full advantage of that hillside nap because, as I was descending from there, I started to feel better, both in my legs and my back. I was able to run again with relative comfort and was able to move forward consistently. Miraculously, when I finally arrived at the next aid station several miles later, I had forty-five minutes until the time cutoff ! That was such a huge relief, I can't even describe it. After grabbing a quick bite, I lay down on the only open spot in the tent, an asphalt bed in front of a blaring television, but it didn't matter. I quickly drifted in and out of real sleep that I so desperately needed. From this point, I started taking a turn for the better, and I was even able to squeeze in one more nap at the next aid station. Physically, I was back to a manageable state.

As the second night gave way to a new day, I was soon presented with a different type of challenge. I had noticed a certain small group of European runners going back and forth with me, as we were running near each other at different points. I kept getting the impression that they were talking about me in their language, especially since I heard one of them say "Americano" when they were far back from me, in a not-so-positive tone. And then they would get quiet as they passed me. Another time, they were behind me as we were going down a particularly technical downhill, and I stumbled slightly. I heard the ring leader say, "Es fragilo."

I'm no linguist, but it certainly felt like he was calling me fragile.

A few minutes later, I decided to confront him about it. I asked in a calm tone what he meant by "fragilo" when he was talking earlier. He was able to speak in English and explained the definition of what fragile means—like glass. I pressed in and asked what he had been talking about. But conveniently, he "didn't remember". I left it at that and tried to not let it put a damper on my experience, but it was still a nagging thought.

A bit later as I was nearing the beginning of another long uphill climb, I felt the presence of the pair of Europeans behind me yet again and felt pressure with them breathing down my neck. Something inside me went off like lightning, and I began to power up this climb like I was racing a trail half marathon. One of the guys stuck with me for a little while as we were going up the switchbacks, repeatedly passing other participants. Eventually, he said, "See you later," as he let me go on up and gave me some space. Not wanting them to catch me, I continued to push all the way up this incline, not knowing where this energy was coming from.

When I passed through an aid station, I only paused long enough to guzzle a cup of whatever liquid was available before moving on. Going down the other side, I kept the heat on my pace and couldn't resist glancing back every now and then. And I think I did catch glimpses of the other guys a ways back when the sight lines opened up. Fortunately, I had created enough space to breathe and was feeling strong enough to keep my momentum up. The silver lining here is that people following me online during UTMB said there were estimated arrival times at certain checkpoints for runner tracking, and one of my times (during this period) was a full hour ahead of the predicted time!

There were only about fifty total Americans at UTMB this year. And luckily, I did have a few positive interactions with a couple of these runners. One guy and I exchanged pleasantries and shared a little running together, and another girl from California showed up at a good time after the unpleasant Europeans. That was a nice way to get my head back in a positive space. Eventually, I was on my own again and working through the final stages, as we were back in France.

I had been warned before the event by my friend Joel (another American from Nashville, who was well ahead of me during this event) that the final climb was the toughest, and the course ending had to be changed this year due to a rock slide. The new climb that was chosen to reroute the course was even tougher than the original climb. With my energy stores lowering again, this definitely felt like it was true. The final climb was really a series of climbs, where it almost seemed like you had peaked out and started to go back down somewhat. The terrain was intense for even a short day hike, sometimes scrambling through bouldery areas. Then you would go back up another steep climb. After several of these that felt very similar, the final push was up a high-grade gravel road, eventually leading up to a ski area up high, where the final aid station awaited weary folks from around the world like myself. My body felt so beaten down when I arrived that I really, really took my time here, since I had several hours left to cover the final downhill 6-ish miles. It was a beautiful view, although somewhat hard to appreciate in such a haggard state.

Tasting that I was near to the finish of this grueling test, I began the slow run down toward Chamonix. There were still other runners around at times, but we had become really spread out at this point. And I was mostly alone here during this hot and sunny afternoon. On this rock-littered section of mountain, it became clear that my feet had taken more than their fair share of stress, and it was superuncomfortable for them to keep taking cushioned blows from each passing stone. As I was counting down the time until I hit smooth pavement in Chamonix, suddenly I encountered my favorite moments during this whole event.

As I rounded a bend in the trail, it opened up to a clearing on the mountainside where there was a bistro, a vibrant place with people outside eating and drinking. The course literally went through the outside seating area, and the people outside were cheering me on with gusto as I was starting to pass through. Their enthusiasm was contagious, and as I was running through, a man held out a glass and said, "Steven, this one is for you!" I honestly felt shocked and honored—I mean you just can't hand out a toast to every one of the hundreds coming through there. I said, "For me?" as he placed it in my hand. The cheers for me got even more animated as I took a long drink, savoring the moment. I took another gulp and was off with a hand wave to acknowledge their support, feeling like I had been treated like a hero.

After a bit more downhill, at long last, the road in Chamonix was beneath my feet again, and I wound my way through town into throngs of crowds lining the streets near the finish. Knowing I was in the homestretch, endorphins took over and tooled up my pace. A blanket of relief surrounded me as I ran the final steps, hardly believing what I had been through. Finally, I crossed over the finish line, and my dream was fully realized. Ultra-Trail du Mont-Blanc, done and done!

After grabbing a drink and a snack in the postrace area, I met another American dude who had completed the event, and it was cool to hang with him for a bit as the finishing ceremonies were going on. I also treated myself to two gelatos, which I had been craving during the final portion of the event.

The following day, my parents arrived in Chamonix, and we had a wonderful time sharing stories and having new experiences in Chamonix, Courmayeur, Paris, and London.

So where will my running take me now? It's been close to a year since UTMB 2018 as I finish this write-up, and I'm still content to run casually and focus more on community, exploration of new places, and general well-being. One thing is for sure: Running ultras, and UTMB in particular, has left me with indelible memories and taught me that perseverance in the face of adversity goes a long way—a very long way.

CHAPTER 20

Post-UTMB Happenings

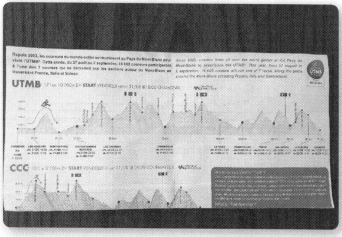

The best part of our trip to England was on Sunday, September 2, when we boarded the Eurostar (the high-speed train that goes under the English Channel from London to Paris). There was a message from Amy (our daughter who was in Tokyo and monitoring Steven's race online). She said that Steven had just finished his race! Then my cell phone showed multiple texts from Steven that he had sent earlier. And I was able to call him and congratulate him (due to good Wi-Fi on the Eurostar). We were so glad to hear his voice and know he was okay!

UTMB is reported to be 171 kilometers in total distance, which is 100 miles. But Steven's GPS watch registered 116 miles at the end. Wow!

At this point, Jay and I were in England and on the train to Europe. But in less than twenty-four hours, and several train rides later, we would see Steven in Chamonix, France, and be able to congratulate him in person. Since it was over

650 miles to Chamonix and late in the afternoon, our travel agent (Sherry from Nashville AAA) had arranged for us to spend the night in Paris and travel by train to Chamonix the next day. This proved to be a great idea, because we learned a lot about Paris in less than twenty-four hours that proved very helpful on our return trip there with Steven a week later.

We were so elated with the news that Steven was finished with his race that, when we got our lunch provided on the Eurostar, it tasted fantastic, and the rest of the trip to Paris seemed like a dream. When we arrived at the train station in Paris, Gare du Nord, we were met by a taxi driver, whose arrival had been prearranged by our travel agent. He held a sign that read, "Avanti McNeal."

I decided to begin using my limited French and said, "Bonjour, monsieur. We are the McNeals."

He smiled and pointed to the right side of the platform to indicate where we were to go. He looked distracted so I said, "Ca va?" which means, "How are you?"

He responded in a positive way by saying, "I'm better now," in English.

That interaction seemed to set the tone for our whole evening in Paris.

Then we got into an elevator down to the van. He helped us load our luggage and drove us up a ramp to the streets of Paris. It was a wow moment when we emerged from the ramp into total traffic and pandemonium. About six to eight lanes merged into three lanes, and all filled with taxis, people on motorcycles and scooters, and more people on bicycles or walking. It was a beautiful Sunday afternoon, and everyone was outside. Our taxi driver said it was always busy after the trains came in.Then the driver said we were his last customers of the day. And would we like to be driven near the Champs-Élysées and the fountains? We said sure! Then he gave us some good advice about being careful to close our jacket pockets when outside in Paris, due to the people picking pockets. He also took us around the park near our hotel and the fountain, and we saw the Eiffel Tower from a distance. Then he pointed out the Tuileries Gardens in front of the Louvre museum. Our hotel was Hotel Cambon in the fashion district, and he told us that Chanel would close soon. I also saw the Tom Ford shop. As I'd been interested in fashion all my life, many of the designer names were familiar.

We said goodbye to our nice taxi driver and asked if we would see him in the morning when we departed for Gare de Lyon train station and got on the train toward Chamonix. He said he couldn't say because a dispatcher would determine who drove us there. I said a prayer for him, and then we entered the hotel. We were checked in by a really nice girl named Manuela. She also arranged a transfer for us to Gare de Lyon the next morning. We went to our room and got changed and then decided to do some walking outside while the sun was still out. So we walked across to the Tuileries Gardens, where we saw several families sitting together and a team of young men playing a game called *pétanque*, which is similar to bocce ball. We also saw a merry-go-round in the park while we walked all the way to the end and then back to our hotel. We could see the glass pyramid that marked the entrance to the Louvre and remembered that our taxi driver had said that the Louvre used to be a royal palace many years ago, from 1202 to the 1500s.

After our walk, we went across the street from our hotel to a restaurant with an open cafe on the street. The maître d' sat us at a table near a couple from Illinois. That couple had been in Paris for two days and shared some good information about the Notre-Dame cathedral. I knew we wanted to go there when we come back to Paris on Sunday, September 9, and Steven would be with us then.

I ordered a croque monsieur sandwich, which was a grilled cheese on French bread. Jay ordered fish with vegetables. Then we had to try a French dessert, so I asked the waiter, "What are the choices?" He listed four dessert choices, and I chose the second one with warm chocolate sauce. They were pastries with ice cream in the middle called profiteroles. The woman next to us said, "You can't go wrong with profiteroles." The dessert was amazing!

We went back to our hotel and went to sleep. We were off to see Steven tomorrow, and we couldn't wait!

The next morning was Monday. We got ready and went downstairs to eat breakfast in the hotel dining room. It was lovely. There were tables already set up with white china plates, silverware, nice placemats, and a crystal glass at each place setting. The breakfast bar was set with hot scrambled eggs, ham, sausage, and bacon. Fresh baguettes, rolls, and croissants accompanied the spread. This was part of our experience on the Cunard Lines ship and most all hotels and restaurants in France, Italy, and London— that everything on the table was able to be cleaned and reused. Their recycling consisted of reusing tableware and being careful to throw paper items in the proper container.

Steven told us he didn't have to look for organic foods in the grocery store in Chamonix because everything was already "organic"—fresh from local farms.

After we ate breakfast, we had arranged for a taxi service to take us to Gare de Lyon train station. Our hotel receptionist told us that our driver was on the way, and she would help us take our luggage outside. I asked if she would mind taking a picture of Jay and me on the sidewalk near the beautiful entrance of our hotel. She seemed very happy to do that, and we had two very good pictures taken there.

When we arrived at the train station, there were hundreds of people all around, and all of the signs were in French. We were in a different world. From our train ticket, I knew we needed to be on the train to Annecy, France, so I watched the screen until it scrolled to that city. It showed that our train would be on platform 19, so we headed there. We got our luggage up on the train and found our seats. It would take about four hours to get to Annecy, and then we'd change trains on our way to Chamonix.

The scenery was beautiful—rolling hills and little villages and lots of sheep and cattle in between! Also, I noticed that most of the houses in the countryside had their own gardens for growing vegetables (mostly tomatoes this time of year). Several homes had clothes drying on racks or clotheslines outside. It was like going back in time, in a good way. After Annecy, we transferred to another train to St. Gervais. Then finally we boarded to a train that would take us to Chamonix and to see Steven. I was texting him, and I let him know that we should be there in forty-five minutes. He texted back, "Yay."

We rode uphill for miles on the last train and then saw

a stop named "Chamonix-Aiguille-du-midi," and we could see the middle of the town in front of us. I showed our train ticket to a lady near us and asked if this was our stop. She nodded yes.

So we got our luggage and got off the train because the train only stays for a few minutes at each stop. We looked at the timetable on the board and realized there was one more stop in Chamonix, and we would have to wait another hour to catch the next train. *So near, except so far away*, we thought.

Steven called me and said he'd looked it up on Google maps and that we were really closer to him and his apartment now than we would have been if we had continued on to the next train stop. Happy accident? Divine intervention? Whatever it was, he said he would walk to meet us in five minutes!

When we saw him walking toward us, it was so good to see him, and he looked wonderful! He wore his blue UTMB finisher vest and a blue shirt! We hugged him and said congratulations in person! It was a very happy day!

We were able to roll our luggage to his apartment, which was a few blocks away.

Then we rested for awhile and saw his beautiful chalet apartment, suggested by his friend Joel. It had a perfect view of Mont Blanc out the back window. Also, it was next door to an elementary school, Ecole de Joan d'Arc. Each afternoon we would hear children playing on the playground. It was so cool.

After talking for awhile, we decided to walk through the town and choose a place to eat dinner. There were a few outdoor cafes, and we chose one with red awnings because it was raining occasionally. It was 2030 (8:30 p.m.). We learned a few things in Europe, among them that European time was like our military time (just like we used when I worked at the hospital). And when eating in a restaurant, you don't want to be in a hurry because every course takes at least thirty minutes to an hour to complete. Steven and I chose pizzas, and Jay ordered a calzone and salad.

While waiting for our food to come, we enjoyed our time together, and Steven talked about the many encounters he'd had during his race the days before. It had only been a few hours since he'd completed the race, and the memories poured out of him.

One of the most intense episodes was the one with two runners who spoke French and ran almost in tandem with him during the second twenty-four hour period of UTMB. One time, they passed Steven on a trail, and he heard them say "fragile." After that exchange, Steven picked up his speed on the next climb. I had been praying during the night and woke up at about 3:30 a.m. to check on his progress. The race report on the UTMB website showed he had increased from 3.8 mph to 4.8 mph. What a way to put those guys behind him.

Another story was a time when he just sat down on a mountain near Courmayeur, Italy, to enjoy the view. A young lady who was running on the trail stopped by him and asked, "Do you want me to take your picture here?" Steven said, "Sure." So now he had a wonderful picture from his favorite place in the race.

After dinner we walked back to his apartment. It was really pretty inside with decorations some might use for Christmas, like reindeer on a bathroom shelf and metal ornaments hanging on the coatrack in the hallway. There were pillows with red and gray and white ski designs on them. It really made the apartment seem like a chalet with the pine walls and floors—especially when we looked outside the back window and saw Mont Blanc in all it's glory there!

We were all so tired that first night, Jay and I from our daylong series of train rides and Steven from only having one night's rest after his three-day race. Steven told us to sleep in a queen-sized bed, and he would sleep on the living room couch. He tucked us into bed and said he loved us and good night. I started crying with relief and held his hand. "That's all I care about," I said, "that you're okay."

He said he knew that.

Then I looked up to see a picture on the wall of a shepherd tending his sheep at the foot of Mont Blanc. I was reminded of Psalm 23 (my favorite psalm), which says, "The Lord is my shepherd, I shall not want." God was with Steven during his race and will always be there for him! Thank you, Jesus.

Tuesday in Chamonix, France, was a day to wash clothes, rest, and plan the rest of the week. For breakfast, Steven asked if I wanted to cook, since he had already gone to the grocery store and gotten eggs, cheese, and bacon. I said that would be great. Jay went to the bakery on the next block and bought a loaf of fresh French bread and two croissants. We also had fresh creamery butter, and I made scrambled eggs and bacon and added thin slices of cheese to the eggs. We had a wonderful meal with a beautiful view of Mont Blanc from the picture window in the dining area. Then Steven talked about his experience in Courmayeur, Italy, and said he would love to go back there sometime. I said that we wanted to see it too and handed him our credit card and said, "That's exciting. Let's see if it's possible."

He spent a few minutes looking at bus schedules to Courmayeur for Wednesday. Steven was able to get bus tickets for us for Wednesday. We went out to dinner later in Chamonix and walked back through the area of the bus station, where we would go the next day.

Believe it or not, it was only a thirty- to forty-minute bus ride—through a tunnel in Mont Blanc and over the mountain and down into Courmayeur, Italy. Steven remembered running through this town about three days before during his UTMB race. The spirit of the people in the town had really inspired him. We got off the bus at the bus station there and then walked up a hill to the main part of town. Steven saw the fluorescent arrows still painted on the streets that had marked his path during the race. He said the runners were told that, if they didn't see the arrows, they were to go back and try to find them so they wouldn't get off the trail. He also saw the concrete staging area where the TV screen that had showed the runners as they came through still remained. Also there was the large white tent that had housed the aid station, still in place.

Across from the staging area were several local restaurants. We chose one that had outdoor seating with red awnings. Jay and Steven ordered cappuccinos, and I got water and just enjoyed looking at the beautiful flowers and several families walking by. The flowers were mostly red geraniums, hot pink roses, and yellow daisies. We walked more, and Steven retraced his steps of some of the race. Then we took his picture at the sign where the runners came through the town. We walked beside several stores and saw beautiful coats, shoes, and dresses, all with designer labels. In one store window, I saw a pair of white designer baby booties that were twenty-two euros (approximately thirty dollars). We didn't buy them, but I did buy a type of Legos made in Switzerland for Zach and Matthew. I hoped they would try to have fun with them. They had started school in Tokyo on August 27—seventh grade for Zach and fifth grade for Matthew—the same week we were on the *Queen Mary II* to England. Steven flew into Amsterdam and then Chamonix. I remembered our call from brother-in-law, Stanley, saying that Steven was probably flying over us that day.

We continued walking around the town of Courmayeur and stopped and got gelato twice, once for gelato, coffee, and cookies. Then later we got gelato after dinner, before we got on the bus back to Chamonix.

Around 4:30 p.m., we started looking for a place to eat dinner before our bus to Chamonix came. We discovered that, in Italy, most restaurants close for several hours during the afternoon and don't reopen until 6:00 p.m. We walked back to the bus station, and Steven asked a waitress at a restaurant there if they were serving pizza. She only spoke Italian, so it seemed like the answer was no. He asked me if I could ask her myself, so we went back to ask her again. When we came around the corner, she was waiting for us. She said, "Pizza?"

It turned out that she had understood and asked the cook and the owner if they could make pizza for us. She took us inside the restaurant and seated us at a nice table near a window. Then she put new white tablecloths on our table and gave us menus. We pointed to the pizzas we wanted to order. Our waitress would say, "Grazie," after each item we ordered. The pizzas were amazing!

I was only able to eat half of my pizza, so I cut it into slices, and our waitress put foil around it. (When we got back to Chamonix, we put the leftover pizza in the refrigerator and actually ate it for lunch on the train to Paris.) We paid our waitress and gave her a very good tip for helping us.

She said, "Grazie mille," over and over, which means "a thousand thanks" or "many thanks." She had saved the day for us. We were able to eat pizza in Italy and then go across the street to get our last gelato for the day before getting on the bus back to Chamonix.

When we were in line to get on the bus, I heard a lady say, "Buona sera." I thought it must mean "good evening" in Italian. So I said, "Buona sera," to the bus driver as we got on the bus. He smiled and said, "Buona sera." It had been one of the best days of our lives! Thank you, God, for this day.

On Friday, we got ready early because it was our day to leave Chamonix and go to Paris. We had arranged transportation with Mountain Drop-offs to come to our apartment at 9:30 a.m. to take us to the train station. When we arrived at the train station, we got on the train to St. Gervais. We ended up sitting beside two couples from Washington, DC, who told us that they were hiking parts of the UTMB trail for eight days. They were taking the train to St. Gervais to hike six miles that day. I told them that Steven had just completed the UTMB 100-mile ultratrail marathon a few days before. Quite excited to hear this, they asked Steven a lot of relevant questions and said they were really glad for him. When we were getting off the train at St. Gervais, one of the men from DC came back toward us and said he wanted to shake Steven's hand. They all congratulated him and told us to have a good day. It was great to see Steven being congratulated for such a great achievement!

We got on another train to Annecy, France, and then onto the last train of the day, the Eurostar train to Paris. At Gare de Lyon in Paris, we got a taxi to Hotel la Bourdonnais, where I had arranged for us to stay. When we got to our hotel, it was dark outside. Julian, the concierge there, told us that our room was only for two people and that the hotel was full. Evidently the travel service I had used hadn't upgraded the room to three people like I had asked. Julian gave us three bottled waters and said he would call another hotel a few blocks away and see if a room was available. In about forty-five minutes, he said the other hotel had a suite for three people with a terrace and a view of the Eiffel Tower! When we got there, the room was on the sixth floor and like a penthouse suite! God answers prayers in a mighty way!

Our room was large, with a forty-eight-inch TV, a king bed, four large chairs, and a beautiful bathroom that smelled like cinnamon. There was a wrought iron balcony outside our window, where we could see the Eiffel Tower was already fully lighted. On other evenings, we noticed that the Eiffel Tower would light in stages over hours until fully lighted by around 8:00 p.m.

Steven had his own room and TV and desk. He "face-planted" on his bed and went to sleep. We were reminded that it had only been a few days since his 100-mile marathon and a long day on trains across France; he needed rest. About 8:30 p.m., Steven said he was ready to go out with us and find a restaurant where we could eat dinner. We walked out the front door of our hotel, turned left, and in a half block saw an italian restaurant, Dell Angelo. Our waiter showed us to a table in front of the main window, which was open to the outside. We ordered our food and loved it. Our waiter said he hoped we would come back, and we did every night!

The next day, we ordered tickets for the Paris hop-on hop-off bus. Then we walked down the street to the right side of our hotel toward the Eiffel Tower, where we would board our bus. It was a beautiful, sunny day, around seventy-two degrees. We were in the park near the Eiffel Tower and took several pictures. After we got on our bus, we rode across the Seine River and toward the Champs-Élysées, the Arc de Triomphe, and the Louvre. We got off the bus at the park near the Louvre. There was a food venue called Pauls that offered quiches and doughnuts and coffee, so we ordered a quiche lorraine (ham and cheese pastry). Steven got a doughnut and coffee, and Jay also ordered a coffee. We sat on a stone wall under a tree and ate our brunch. Then we walked to get in line for the Louvre. It was just a security line check at first, and the guard asked me to remove my "booty pack" (the French term for fanny pack?). Ha ha.

After security, we went down an escalator to the ground floor of the Louvre. Jay and Steven got in two separate queues to buy tickets. The museum was having a glitch in its computer system, and not all lines would continue to be able to purchase tickets. Steven got through first and bought our tickets to get in. I had gotten a museum map (in English). The museum offered versions printed in several different languages. FYI, on the tour bus, you could choose from twelve different languages for the headphone translation.

We looked at our options. I knew that I wanted to see

the *Mona Lisa*, so we went upstairs about four flights to see it. There were about a hundred people in the room getting as close as the velvet ropes would allow to the *Mona Lisa*. We waited for an opening. Then Steven took my picture with the *Mona Lisa* in the background. We also saw the Venus de Milo statue in the Grecian room—along with many other beautiful paintings and sculptures. We even saw some "money"—coins from Ramses III, around 1200 BC. It was a very warm day, and we went downstairs to the "basement" of the Louvre. There were many large stones that comprised the foundation of the Louvre. It was so nice and cool there. Steven was very interested in construction and enjoyed walking around.

When we were finished, we walked out of the Louvre and up the stairs to the gardens. Those gardens connected to the Tuileries Gardens, which were across from the hotel where we had stayed previously. We walked in the shade under the trees the whole length of those gardens. Then we crossed the busy street to Le Comptoir, the restaurant where we'd had dinner a week before. I ordered a croque monsieur sandwich. Jay ordered fish. And Steven ordered Caesar salad with salmon. Then, for dessert, we ordered profiteroles, puff pastries and ice cream with warm chocolate sauce. Our waitress said she could put the sauce on the pastry for us. She held the pitcher of sauce about a foot above the pastry and poured with a flourish. She said, "like Picasso."

We just had time to get back to a bus stop and get to the Notre-Dame cathedral before the afternoon was over. So we walked to the nearest stop a couple of blocks away. When we arrived at a corner near the cathedral, there were several hundred people in the courtyard in front. We saw French military police patrolling there too. The line of people to get into the cathedral was about three hundred feet long. I knew we had a limited time before we had to be back on the bus to go to our hotel.

Steven looked at me and said "Do you want to get in line and try to see if we can get in the entrance in time?"

"Yes," I replied.

The line moved forward constantly, so we were good to go. As we approached the front entrance and climbed the steps, we heard the bells of Notre-Dame begin ringing the half hour; it was 6:30 p.m. As we entered the massive wooden front door, the pipe organ began sounding a glorious hymn. It was amazing! Tears filled my eyes as I realized that we were there in time to see a Saturday evening Mass. We walked to the right side of the sanctuary, where we stood near a wooden railing and watched candles being lit by teenage choir boys in white robes. Then two soloists, a man and a woman, each sang their part of a beautiful hymn in French. They wore dark blue robes and had professional voices. Then the archbishop came forward to begin his sermon.

We had walked by several alcoves where people were lighting candles in red votive holders and saying prayers for their loved ones. There was a separate alcove with a marble statue of Joan of Arc. Our nightly waiter, Kevin, told us that Joan of Arc had gone to another church in Paris called La Madeleine church. Joan of Arc died for her faith in God. She is a very revered saint in France. The school next door to Steven's apartment in Chamonix was named after her, Ecole du Jeanne d'Arc.

After listening to the service for a while longer, we were able to take a few pictures and listen to more beautiful music. Then we left to get on the bus and go to our hotel. Dinner that night was at Dell Angelo, our italian restaurant. We were seated at the same table as the evening before. Our waiter, Kevin, greeted us. We ordered our dinner then and, later, also a dessert to share. We were so full. But when we were going to leave some on our plate, Kevin said with a smile, "You have to eat it all." So we did. A wonderful day in Paris!

Our last day in Paris, we decided to walk around the streets near our hotel and take in the culture. We ate lunch at a sidewalk cafe, bought souvenirs, and got some Paris Starbucks mugs for Steven. The Starbucks coffee was good too.

That evening, we ate dinner at Dell Angelos for the last time. After we ate, we asked Kevin to take our picture. Then we said goodbye. And as I hugged him and kissed his face, he said, "In France, we kiss twice."

So I kissed him on the other side and said, "God bless you." I would be praying for him.

Steven and I walked back to our hotel with our arms around each other's waist, with Jay beside us. We had a great time in Paris!

The next day, we rode to London on the Eurostar train and had a wonderful lunch with a beignet pastry for dessert. Yes, we got entirely spoiled in France eating the country's delicious food. We disembarked in London at St. Pancras train station—which meant that we had come full circle in two weeks' time, from London to Paris to Chamonix and then back to Paris and London. What a whirlwind. So fun!

We got in line for a taxi to our hotel, Lancaster Gate, near Hyde Park and Kensington Palace. Since our room wasn't ready yet, we walked to Hyde Park and got an ice cream cone. We sat on a park bench and enjoyed looking at the flowers and the Serpentine pond. The flowers and fountains were absolutely beautiful.

Then we went back to our hotel and checked into our room.

We bought tickets for the Big Bus of London for the next day. That way, we would be able to get off and on at different stops along the way. Then we walked outside and went to a local pub called The Swan. A girl directed us upstairs to a lovely deck outside. We sat in gray wicker chairs, and a waitress came and took our orders. I ordered fish and chips with mashed peas. The fish was battered and cooked perfectly. It was the best fish I had in London. After dinner, we walked through the streets and then back to the hotel for the night.

The next day, we ate breakfast and then went to the nearest bus stop to catch the Big Bus. Steven and I were able to sit on the top deck of the bus and hear the young lady who told the historical facts of the locations we were seeing as we passed. When we got to Trafalgar Square, there was a large statue of Lord Nelson, a great British admiral. She said before there were celebrities and movie stars, we had war heroes. Lord Nelson was England's greatest war hero of his time. Under his leadership, the British Navy won four major battles. The last battle was the one at Trafalgar. After the battle was over, Lord Nelson was standing on the deck of his ship, and a French sniper shot him. As he lay there dying, he said, "Thank God I have done my duty." His body was brought back to London for his funeral. It was a very inspiring story.

We rode on the bus until we got to a train station near Westminster Chapel. Then we found a nice restaurant for lunch. We all had hamburgers and fries. Steven was still hungry, so he ordered brownies with pistachio ice cream for dessert. He shared some of it with us, and it tasted wonderful. After we ate, we took pictures near one of the famous red telephone booths. I think Steven was still recovering from his race because he wanted to go back to our hotel and rest. He would lie down (face-plant) on the bed as soon as he got to the room.

For dinner, we walked out of our hotel and turned left onto a side road. Within a block, we saw an Italian restaurant called Taormina, which ended up being our favorite restaurant in London. We ordered our dinners then had tiramisu for dessert. It was delicious!

On Wednesday, since we had already purchased tickets to tour Kensington Palace, we decided to walk through the park to the palace instead of taking a bus. The route we took was through several city blocks past our hotel where we passed scores of people walking toward buses, trains, and taxis and riding bicycles. The weather was about fifty-five degrees and cloudy. We crossed the final intersection and entered the park, where there were families near a pond with ducks; many people walked dogs and pushed strollers. Then we reached the famous statue of Queen Victoria, which had been commissioned by her daughter Beatrice. It was near the sidewalk that led to the main entrance of the palace. The younger royal families, Prince William and Prince Harry's, were in residence there, but we didn't see any of them while we were there.

We walked up to the main entrance and were directed

to the line where we would enter the palace. Everyone was very friendly. We went through the security line and walked inside, where a young lady was handing out maps of the inside of the palace. She told us we might want to see the Princess Diana exhibit soon, because it would get crowded later on in the day. Her dresses were on display to the right and up the stairs. On the left side of the entrance were the former king and queen's private apartments, dating from the 1700s. She said there would be a lecture about Queen Victoria's life in the main dining room upstairs at 11:00 a.m. Since Jay and I had seen the first year of the Victoria series on *Masterpiece* on BBC, I was really interested to hear that lecture.

We decided to take the young lady's advice and went up three flights of stairs to see Diana's dresses first. There were four rooms with dresses behind glass walls in each room. In the first room was the black velvet dress Diana had worn when she danced with John Travolta at the white house in the 1980s. I saw many more dresses that I recognized. Also, there was a saying on one of the walls—"There will only ever be one Diana." She always identified herself with those who were suffering or oppressed.

The next part of the palace we visited were the Victorian apartments. We saw one of Albert's (Victoria's husband) uniforms. Also on display was one of Victoria's dresses, which looked like a child's dress since she was only 4 foot eleven. Victoria was only eighteen years old when she became queen of England and the British Empire. At the lecture, the speaker told us that Victoria was born at Kensington Palace and met her husband, Prince Albert, there. She was not allowed to walk downstairs by herself and had to hold someone's hand because her family was afraid she would fall. Her mother slept in her room until the day she became queen at age eighteen. Literally, her first command was that her mother be sent to the opposite side of the palace to have an apartment there. I think she was more than ready to have her own privacy.

Julian, the lecturer told us that Queen Victoria had nine children, and all of them married crowned rulers of different countries in Europe. She lived to be in her eighties and celebrated her diamond jubilee, sixty years, as queen of England. After the lecture, I talked with a really nice lady who was a hostess at the palace. I told her that the lecturer had done an excellent job of making it interesting and humorous. I also told her we had seen the Victoria series on BBC. She said she would tell Julian we were impressed, and it would mean so much to him.

After talking to her, we went downstairs to see the royal apartments. Next, we headed out through the gift shop and gardens. Then we walked toward our hotel. It was raining now, so we stopped to eat lunch and then to another shop to get gelato.

When we finally got to our hotel, we rested. Then Steven made reservations at the Island Grill, a restaurant a few blocks from our hotel. This would be our last night together on our vacation. While we were waiting for our food at the dinner table that evening, Steven looked at me and said, "Thank you for paying for my entry fee for the UTMB and encouraging me to go to the race."

With tears in my eyes, I said, "You're so welcome. During the race, I'd been afraid I might have made the wrong decision—if something had gone wrong in the race. But I was so glad you made it through!"

We had a wonderful meal together.

The next day, Steven flew back to Oregon. And a few days later, we boarded the *Queen Mary II* and went to New York City and then back home to Georgia. There really is no place like home.

EPILOGUE

It's been a year since the 2018 Ultra-Trail du Mont-Blanc where Steven ran, hiked, jogged, walked, and sometimes stumbled 100 miles plus through the Alps and three countries (France, Italy, and Switzerland and back to France). There are more than eleven uphill climbs on the race course map, some over 8,000 feet above sea level. For instance, Grand Col Ferret (several miles past the halfway point of the race) at the border of Italy and Switzerland has an elevation of 2,490 meters or 8,169 feet. This pass separates the Mont Blanc Massif from the Pennine Alps.

Steven moved to Oregon in summer 2017, specifically to train and prepare for the Mountain Lakes 100 mile race in order to qualify for UTMB.

As often happens when we're preparing for events in life, God handed Steven more challenges. After he completed the Mountain Lakes 100 at Olallie Lake in Oregon in September 2017, he found out that he needed to find a new place to live. Being an owner of a condo and a house located in Nashville, Steven felt he didn't want to rent if he could find an affordable place to buy. He was living in Bend, Oregon, at the time and couldn't find a place there but did find a cabin in La Pine, Oregon, thirty miles south of Bend.

In November 2017, he became owner of an A-frame cabin in La Pine, Oregon. He sent us a picture of him sitting on the front porch of the cabin. But this was only the beginning, because the A-frame was unlivable due to the former owners having had a fire in the wood-burning fireplace that went out of control and up the front wall. Plus, there was no bathroom, no heat or air, and no running water. What?

Steven's solution was to buy a six-foot-by-six-foot shed and have it delivered to his property in Oregon before bad weather came in winter. He had a sleeping bag that was certified to protect for temperatures to twenty degrees below zero. And he was going to sleep on the floor of the shed. I knew that this was a bad idea, but he was an adult, so all I could do was give my opinion (for what it's worth) and pray, pray, pray that he would find another solution. That solution came in the form of his landlady at the Airbnb he was staying in for a few days, Ms. Linda. She found out his plans for living in a shed and told him that she had been through several winters in Oregon. She said the winters could be very severe, with feet of snow. So I suggested he live in an RV while he was renovating the cabin. When he went to an RV dealer, he found out that it was possible to have it moved to his property and live in it. Turns out he lived in the RV for fifteen months until his A-frame was ready. He hired a contractor, Eric, and worked alongside him during most of those fifteen months.

So, let's see. Steven was simultaneously training for UTMB, working on his cabin, and living in an RV. I'd always known he was resourceful, and this was just part of all the challenges he faced at this time. That he completed the UTMB still seems like a dream to me. (Steven did have a wall of pictures in his house in Nashville, which included Mont Blanc. He called it his "dream wall.")

As of 2019, one year past his race in France, Steven is currently renovating his house in Nashville to put it on the market. More improvements to his cabin in Oregon are on standby until he can get back there, hopefully, in September.

In June, he did paint and make cabinet doors for the bathrooms of his condo and has it available for rent again. He still runs almost daily with his running groups in Nashville and Seattle. Oh yes, did I mention he went to a party last year given by a friend for a running group in Nashville and, quite possibly, met the love of his life?! She has a new job in Seattle—hence, the running group in Seattle. Prayers of many years are being fulfilled daily.

With God all things are possible.

Matthew 19:26—NKJV

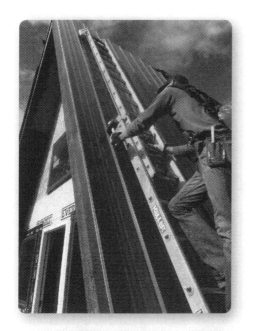

ABOUT THE AUTHOR

J ennie McNeal has been a medical technologist in hospital laboratories for over 40 years. She has enjoyed reading books and writing journals for the last several years. Since retiring from lab work over one year ago, she has written her first book about her son's journey as an ultramarathon runner. Her son, Steven, lives in Oregon and has run in over 20 ultramarathons, including four 100 mile races. Steven's own blog posts are included in this book.

Jennie is a wife, mother of two and a grandmother of two wonderful grandsons.

She lives in Georgia with her husband, Jay. They have been married for 47 years.

Printed in the United States
By Bookmasters